MW00809242

Reading Comprehension

Teacher Created Materials

Publisher:
Rachelle Cracchiolo, M.S. Ed.

Editor-in-Chief:
Sharon Coan, M.S. Ed.

Project Managers:
Maria Elvira Gallardo, M.A.
Marcia Russell, M.A. Ed.

Photo Credits:
Photos.com—All except:
Bookmatrix—p. 5
TCM staff—p. 97
Library of Congress—
pp. 117, 125
Corel—pp. 69, 106, 109
iStockphoto—pp. 49, 57, 81,
106

Art Director:
Lee Aucoin

Designer:
Lesley Palmer

Product Developers:
Teacher Created Materials
Creative Services, Inc.

Product Manager:
Phil Garcia

To order additional copies of this book or any other Teacher Created Materials products, go to www.tcmpub.com or call 1-800-858-7339.

Teacher Created Materials
5301 Oceanus Drive
Huntington Beach, CA 92649-1030
www.tcmpub.com
ISBN 978-1-4258-0089-5
©2006 Teacher Created Materials, Inc.
Reprinted 2012

No part of this publication may be copied, transmitted, stored, or recorded in any form without written permission from the publisher.

Table of Contents

Introduction 4

Mandy the Mammal 5

The Experiment 9

Spider Pets 13

The Seasons 17

Something Is Following Me 21

Flags of the World 25

Can You Taste That? 29

Transportation 33

The Castle 37

Amazing Reptiles 41

Pencil Problems 45

Working Dogs 49

Friends for Peachy 53

Going West to California 57

Changes 61

Alligator or Crocodile? 65

The Big Day 69

A Little Bit of Sand 73

Game Time 77

Mac Makes a Difference 81

The Oceans 85

The Sun 89

Community Helpers 93

The Spelling Bee 97

The Land of the Rising Sun 101

What Makes an Insect an Insect 105

All Kinds of Families 109

The Ball Game 113

The Lady with the Lamp 117

Top of the World 121

Martin Luther King, Jr. 125

George Washington 129

Comprehension Review 133

Introduction to Reading Comprehension

The lessons in this book will help you learn to understand what you read. Each lesson has a selection to read. Then you work with skills to help you understand what you read. Each lesson ends with a practice activity that helps you see what you know about the selection.

You can use these steps to help you as you work in the book. For each selection, follow these steps.

1. Read the Before Reading questions.

Before Reading
- Do you have brothers or sisters?
- How are you alike or different from your siblings?

2. Think about what you already know about the subject.

3. Read the selection. Use the During Reading questions.

During Reading
- How did the brothers get along?
- How would you feel about moving?

4. Review the selection using the After Reading questions.

After Reading
- Are there more than these kinds of bikes?
- Which kind of bike would you like to have?

5. Summarize and apply the information. Complete the activities in the book.

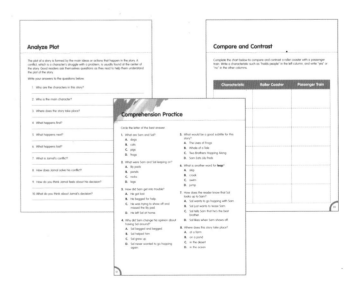

After completing all the activities, use the Comprehension Review section to review the information presented in the book. These pages also help you to check up on your skills.

Mandy the Mammal

Before Reading

- What is a mammal?
- How do you feel on the first day of school?

During Reading

- What kind of mammal is born from an egg?
- Is Bobby the bear a mammal?

After Reading

- Is a person a mammal?
- What other animals are mammals?

Vocabulary

mammal: a large group of animals with backbones that feed their young with milk

pouch: the part of an animal that is like a sack or pocket

Monday was Mandy's first day of school. She loved school and her new lunchbox. Mandy's teacher asked the students to tell the class about themselves.

Mandy was the first student to talk. She said, "Hi, my name is Mandy. I'm a mammal. Mammals have hair. Most mammals eat plants. Some eat meat. Some eat plants and meat."

Her teacher then asked, "Are there any other mammals in this room?"

Seven mammals raised their hands. "I am a mammal too," said Miss Tiger. "Some mammals like platypuses come out of eggs. Other mammals like kangaroos are born early and live in a pouch. I lived in my mom's belly until I was born," she told the class. "This is how most mammals are born."

Bobby the bear said, "They can be tall or short. Some are fast and others are slow." He then asked, "Mandy, what kind of mammal are you?"

Mandy smiled and said, "I am a moose!"

Visualize

Reread the selection, visualizing what Mandy and her classroom would have looked like. In the space below, draw a picture of what you think the classroom, students, and teacher look like. When you finish the picture, check your picture against the selection. Then describe your picture on the lines below.

_____

_____

_____

_____

_____

_____

© Teacher Created Materials

Analyze Plot Structure

The plot is what happens at the beginning, middle, and end of a story. By "Beginning," write about what happened at the beginning of the story. By "Middle," write about what happened in the middle of the story. By "End," write about what happened at the end of the story.

Beginning _____

_____

_____

_____

Middle _____

_____

_____

_____

_____

End _____

_____

_____

_____

Comprehension Practice

Circle the letter of the best answer.

1. All mammals only eat plants.
   A. True
   B. False

2. Kangaroos are mammals.
   A. True
   B. False

3. Mandy and Bobby are not mammals.
   A. True
   B. False

4. All mammals are short and slow.
   A. True
   B. False

5. Which of the following is NOT true?
   A. Tigers, kangaroos, and bears are all mammals.
   B. Mandy is the only mammal in her class.
   C. Bobby the bear is a mammal.
   D. There are many kinds of mammals.

6. What is a **pouch**?
   A. where kangaroo babies live
   B. a kind of lunchbox
   C. something bright green
   D. an egg

7. When do you learn Mandy is a moose?
   A. at the beginning of the story
   B. Mandy never says what she is
   C. at the end of the story
   D. Mandy is not a moose.

8. What did Bobby look like?
   A. small and pink
   B. large and covered with hair
   C. tall with big antlers
   D. striped

#50089 Reading Comprehension—Level D   © *Teacher Created Materials*

The Experiment

Before Reading

- What is an experiment?
- Have you ever conducted an experiment?

During Reading

- What was the purpose of Margo's experiment?
- What materials did Margo use for her experiment?

After Reading

- How did Margo show what makes day and night?
- How long does it take Earth to spin all the way around?

Margo couldn't wait to get home from school. She had an experiment to try. She was going to show her mom what makes day and night!

First, she gathered the materials she needed. She needed a globe, some clay, and a bright light. She set the lamp about a foot away from the globe. Then she stuck a piece of clay on the globe. "That's us!" she told her mom.

Next, she turned on the light. She shined it on the globe. "We'll pretend the light is the sun," she said. "See how it's shining on the clay? That means it's daytime where we are."

Then she spun the globe around halfway. "Watch what happens now!" she said. "As Earth rotates, the clay rotates with it. Eventually, it moves out of the light. See, the light isn't shining on us anymore. Now it's nighttime for us, and daytime for the people on the other side of Earth!"

The experiment was a success. And Margo finally understood what makes day and night.

Vocabulary

experiment: an activity to find out how something works

globe: a model of Earth

rotate: to spin

Ask Questions

As you read "The Experiment," you can ask and answer questions. They will help you understand the story. Answer these questions. Find the answers in the story.

1. What does the light in the experiment represent?

_____

_____

2. What does the clay represent?

_____

_____

3. Why does Margo spin the globe?

_____

_____

4. What happens on Earth as it rotates?

_____

_____

5. What was the purpose of Margo's experiment?

_____

_____

Identify Sequence

In the story "The Experiment," Margo conducts an experiment. The steps she followed are listed below. As you read the story, think about the order of the steps. Write the steps in the order Margo does them.

shine light on globe to model sunlight

gather materials

spin globe to show how Earth changes from day to night

stick clay on globe

Step 1

_____

Step 2

_____

Step 3

_____

Step 4

_____

Comprehension Practice

Circle the letter of the best answer.

1. Which item was NOT used in the experiment?
   A. a light
   B. a piece of string
   C. a globe
   D. clay

2. What did the clay represent?
   A. Margo and her mom's location
   B. the North Pole
   C. the sun
   D. an island

3. What did the light represent?
   A. the moon
   B. Jupiter
   C. gravity
   D. the sun

4. How did Margo model Earth rotating?
   A. by moving the light around the globe
   B. by moving the globe around the light
   C. by spinning the globe
   D. by spinning the light

5. Which main idea tells why Margo's experiment was a success?
   A. Margo had fun doing her experiment.
   B. Margo's mom liked her experiment.
   C. It helped her understand day and night.
   D. It showed where she lived on the globe.

6. Why is a **globe** round?
   A. It is easier to spin if it is round.
   B. The sun is round.
   C. Round is prettier than square.
   D. It models Earth and Earth is nearly round.

7. What makes day and night happen on Earth?
   A. Earth moves around the sun.
   B. The sun moves around Earth.
   C. The sun stays in one place and Earth rotates.
   D. A huge dog swallows the sun every night.

8. Which of these things did Margo do last?
   A. She spun the globe around halfway.
   B. She stuck clay on the globe.
   C. She gathered materials.
   D. She turned on the light.

 #50089 Reading Comprehension—Level D   © *Teacher Created Materials*

Spider Pets

On Saturday morning Billy played outside while his dad mowed the lawn. Billy liked to play outside. He liked to play in the mud and dig holes. Today when Billy was playing in the mud, he saw a spider! He let it crawl into his jar. Billy had a new pet.

This spider was black and yellow. As he looked at it, Billy saw that the spider had eight legs and two body parts. Billy needed to know more about the spider, so he asked his dad. Dad told Billy that the spider makes its own web. The spider lives near the web. Billy's dad said that the spider eats bugs. It catches them in its web. Dad said spiders lay eggs, and most enclose them in sacs.

Billy liked the spider but knew it had its own home. He knew what he had to do with the spider.

Before Reading

- What is a spider?
- Is a spider a good pet?

During Reading

- Where did Billy put the spider?
- How many legs do spiders have?

After Reading

- What kind of spider did Billy find?
- Why do spiders make webs?

Vocabulary

spider: a small animal with eight legs

lawn: land covered with grass

web: a net of tiny threads spun by a spider

sacs: bags spiders make with web thread

Predict

Many stories that you will read do not tell you everything that happens. The author wants you to make your own prediction of what happens. Answer the questions by making a prediction of what you think might have happened.

What do you think Billy's friends would say about keeping the spider as a pet?

_____

_____

_____

_____

_____

_____

The story ends by saying Billy liked the spider but knew it had its own home. He knew what he had to do with the spider. What do you think Billy did with the spider?

_____

_____

_____

_____

_____

_____

Identify Main Idea and Supporting Details

The following is a main idea web. The word **Spiders** in the center circle is the main topic of the web. In the other circles, add the information you learned about spiders from the story. Your answers should be short.

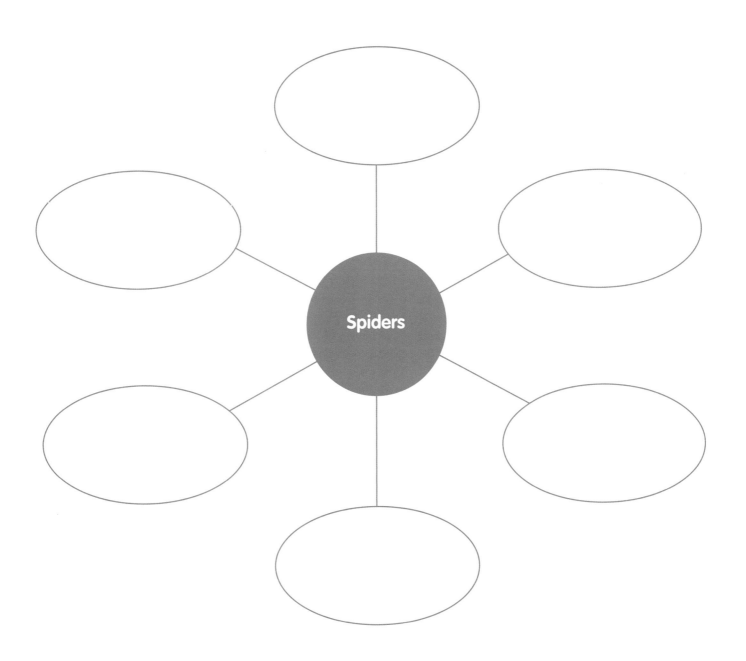

Comprehension Practice

Circle the letter of the best answer.

1. Where does the spider catch food?
   A. on the bottom of the ocean
   B. in a web
   C. in a jar
   D. in the house

2. Where does Billy keep the spider after he catches it?
   A. in his bedroom
   B. under his bed
   C. in a jar
   D. in his hand

3. What did the spider look like?
   A. It was black and yellow and had eight legs and two body parts.
   B. It was big and hairy with spots.
   C. The spider was so small Billy didn't know what it looked like.
   D. The spider was brown.

4. What do you think Billy did with the spider at the end of the story?
   A. He kept the spider in the jar in his room.
   B. He gave the spider to his dad.
   C. He let the spider go.
   D. Billy's dog ate the spider.

5. Which is the main point of this story?
   A. It tells us many interesting things about spiders.
   B. Saturday is a good day to mow the lawn.
   C. Spiders make good pets.
   D. Billy likes to dig holes and play in the mud.

6. What is a **sac**?
   A. a kind of nest
   B. a jar
   C. a place where spiders keep their eggs
   D. a kind of book bag

7. What do spiders eat?
   A. leaves
   B. bugs
   C. their own webs
   D. many different things

8. What will the spider do if Billy lets it go?
   A. It will follow Billy around.
   B. It will build another web and catch bugs to eat.
   C. It will look for another jar to live in.
   D. It will move into Billy's house.

#50089 Reading Comprehension—Level D
© Teacher Created Materials

The Seasons

Each year has four seasons. The seasons are winter, spring, summer, and fall. Each season has a different kind of weather. Areas of the country can have different weather in each season.

During the winter it can get very cold outside. Many people have to wear heavy coats and hats. In some parts of the world, snow falls from the sky. Some animals hide in the winter.

Spring comes after winter. The weather starts to get warm. Plants begin to grow. Spring is when school usually ends and summer begins.

Winter

In the summer it is very warm. People like to swim. Animals like to stay outside all day. The summer is a time for things to grow.

The next season is fall. This is the time when school begins in many places! Leaves change color. The leaves fall from the trees. The air starts to get cold, and people wear jackets.

There are many different things that change during each season. What season do you like best?

Spring

Summer

Fall

Before Reading

- What is a season?
- How many times do the seasons change each year?

During Reading

- What is one way to determine if it is fall?
- What season is it at the end of most school years?

After Reading

- What season is it now where you live?
- Are seasons the same in all parts of the world? Why or why not?

Vocabulary

season: one of the four times of the year

weather: the outside air and its temperature, wind, and other things

Classify/Categorize

Grouping things together that are the same or that describe a specific topic is called classifying or categorizing. Think about the different things that happen during each season and write the information in the column that matches its season.

Winter	Spring	Summer	Fall

                    © Teacher Created Materials

Make Inferences

You can use what you already know to form ideas about what you read in "The Seasons." Think about what the story tells you. Draw conclusions about which season is described. Circle the name of the season.

1. This is Rico's favorite time of year. He gathers red and yellow leaves. He puts the leaves on his bulletin board. The family works together to rake the leaves and bag them. What season is Rico's favorite season?

   Spring   Summer   Fall   Winter

2. Shelley has on her warm jacket. She has on her hat and mittens. She and Jacqui are pulling a sled through the snow. They will take the sled to the top of the hill and ride it down. It is fun to slide through the snow. What season is it?

   Spring   Summer   Fall   Winter

3. It is very hot in the sun. Dad is sweating as he mows the lawn. Mom is watching Alyssa. She is playing in a wading pool. Dad comes over to the pool. He puts his feet in. He and Alyssa wade together on this hot day. What season is it?

   Spring   Summer   Fall   Winter

4. Today I saw a bird in the yard. I think it was a robin. Now the trees have tiny leaves on them. The grass is getting green. Some tulips are in bloom. The flowers are yellow, red, white, and pink. What season is it?

   Spring   Summer   Fall   Winter

Comprehension Practice

Circle the letter of the best answer.

1. In which season is it most likely to snow?
   A. winter
   B. spring
   C. summer
   D. fall

2. How many times do the seasons change each year?
   A. one
   B. two
   C. three
   D. four

3. During which season does school usually begin?
   A. winter
   B. spring
   C. summer
   D. fall

4. During which season do plants begin to grow again?
   A. winter
   B. spring
   C. summer
   D. fall

5. This story is mainly about _____.
   A. snow falling
   B. people going swimming
   C. plants beginning to grow
   D. the changes that we see with different seasons

6. Which is NOT a type of **weather**?
   A. rain
   B. wind
   C. night
   D. snow

7. Which statement is NOT true?
   A. It snows in the winter in every part of the world.
   B. There are four seasons—winter, spring, summer, and fall.
   C. In many places, the weather is different in the different seasons.
   D. Animals do different things in the summer and the winter.

8. People are more likely to wear swimsuits in which season?
   A. summer
   B. winter
   C. fall
   D. spring

© *Teacher Created Materials*

Something Is Following Me

Lindsay and her big sister Jenny took their dog for a walk. Lindsay's dog's name is Max. The three walked up and down the streets while Max stopped and smelled the flowers.

When Lindsay turned to go to the park, she felt like she was being followed. When she turned around, she didn't see anything. Lindsay kept walking, but she still felt like something was there. Lindsay told Jenny how she felt, and Jenny began to laugh.

Lindsay said, "Why are you laughing at me?"

"Look at Max. He is being followed too!" Jenny told her.

As Lindsay looked down at Max, she saw what was following him. It was the same thing that was following her. In fact, it follows everyone. It was a shadow!

Before Reading

- What do you think the story is about based on the title?
- Have you ever walked behind someone?

During Reading

- Where are Lindsay and her sister going?
- What is following Lindsay, Jenny, and Max?

After Reading

- Can you see your shadow at night?
- Is your shadow always behind you?

Vocabulary

street: a road in a city or town, usually with buildings on both sides

shadow: shade made by a person, animal, or thing

park: land set aside for pleasure

Analyze Plot Structure

Fill in the chart. Identify the plot (what happens in the story) of this selection. Plot moves the story from beginning to middle to end.

Beginning _____

_____

_____

_____

Middle _____

_____

_____

_____

_____

_____

End _____

_____

_____

_____

Visualize

Reread the selection, visualizing how Lindsay, Jenny, Max, and their shadows look. In the space below, draw a picture of what you think they look like. Describe your picture on the lines below.

_____

_____

_____

_____

_____

Comprehension Practice

Circle the letter of the best answer.

1. Who is Max?
   A. Lindsay's brother
   B. Lindsay's friend
   C. A man on the street
   D. Lindsay's dog

2. Why does Lindsay's sister laugh at her when she says that something is following them?
   A. She thinks it is a joke.
   B. She doesn't laugh.
   C. She knows what is following them.
   D. She thinks her sister is seeing things.

3. What is following Lindsay?
   A. her dog
   B. her mother
   C. her father
   D. her shadow

4. Why is her shadow following her?
   A. Her shadow was mad at her.
   B. Her shadow is a shade made by her body as she walks.
   C. Jenny told the shadow to follow her.
   D. They don't know why the shadow is following them.

5. How do you think Lindsay feels when she finds out what is following her?
   A. relieved
   B. happy
   C. angry
   D. sad

6. Think about the meaning of **park**. Is it a good place for Lindsay, Jenny, and Max to walk?
   A. No, parks have too many shadows.
   B. No, because children and dogs can't go there.
   C. Yes, a park is set aside as a nice place for people to enjoy.
   D. Yes, there are dogs there for Max to fight with.

7. When does the reader learn what is following Lindsay?
   A. It is never mentioned in the story.
   B. in the middle of story
   C. in the second sentence
   D. at the very end of the story

8. What would you see if you were with Lindsay on her walk?
   A. a dog
   B. flowers
   C. shadows
   D. all of the above

Flags of the World

What colors will you find on national flags? Most countries have flags with at least two of eight colors. The colors are yellow, orange, red, black, white, brown, blue, and green. The one-color flag of Libya is different. This flag is solid green.

Many flags have stripes that are vertical. The three stripes on the flag of Italy go up and down. The stripes are green, white, and red. Some flags have horizontal stripes. The three stripes on the flag of Russia go side to side. The stripes are white, blue, and red from top to bottom.

Italy

Russia

Some flags have symbols on them. Stars are a popular symbol on flags. The Congo and Chinese flags have stars. Crescents and stars together are seen on many flags too. The flag of Turkey has one star and one crescent.

Some flags have stripes and symbols. The flag of Canada has red, white, and red stripes that go up and down. In the middle of the white stripe is a large maple leaf. The flag of Lebanon has horizontal red, white, and red stripes. The flag has a cedar tree in the middle of the white stripe.

Think of your country's flag. What does it look like? Does it have stripes? Does it have symbols? Find out what the symbols and colors of your flag stand for.

Before Reading

- What is a flag?
- What does your country's flag look like?

During Reading

- What colors are most national flags?
- How does the Libyan flag differ from others?

After Reading

- Where do you see your country's flag displayed?
- Why do nations proudly display their flags?

Vocabulary

crescent: the shape of the moon in its first or last quarter

horizontal: straight across from side to side

vertical: straight up and down

Compare and Contrast

We can compare and contrast things by telling how they are alike and how they are different. As you read "Flags of the World," think about how the flags of Russia and Italy are alike. Think about how they are different. Use the information to complete the Venn diagram.

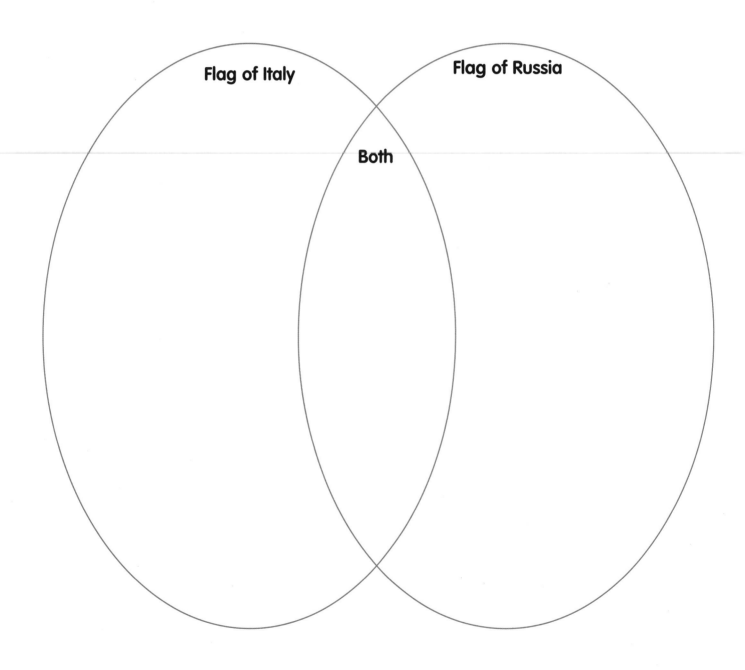

Flag of Italy

Flag of Russia

Both

 © *Teacher Created Materials*

Visualize

In the selection "Flags of the World," the author describes flags of the world. As you read the selection, make a picture in your mind of what some of the flags look like. Then, use colored pens or pencils to draw the flags below using the pictures in your mind.

What does the flag of Lebanon look like? Draw a picture.

What does the Canadian flag look like? Draw a picture.

Comprehension Practice

Circle the letter of the best answer.

1. Which color are you not likely to find on a flag?
   A. orange
   B. pink
   C. blue
   D. brown

2. Which of these flags has horizontal stripes?
   A. flag of Italy
   B. flag of Libya
   C. flag of Russia
   D. flag of Canada

3. How many stripes are on the Russian flag?
   A. two
   B. three
   C. four
   D. five

4. What is true of all flags?
   A. All flags have color.
   B. All flags have horizontal stripes.
   C. All flags have vertical stripes.
   D. All flags have stars or crescents.

5. What do you think after reading this article?
   A. All countries have flags.
   B. Only very large countries have flags.
   C. Only a few countries have flags.
   D. Most countries have flags.

6. Stripes that are **horizontal** go _____.
   A. side to side
   B. up and down
   C. in waves
   D. in circles

7. What is the same about the US flag and the flag of Russia?
   A. both are green
   B. both have only three stripes
   C. both are red, white, and blue
   D. neither one has stripes

8. The flag of Canada has stripes that are _____.
   A. vertical
   B. horizontal
   C. green and blue
   D. round

Can You Taste That?

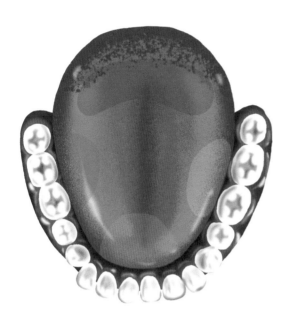

Before Reading

- What things taste good to you?
- What things taste bad to you?

What exactly does your tongue do when you take a bite of food? It goes through a lot of work to tell you if you like something or not!

Taste buds on your tongue are in groups called papillae. These groups are connected to nerves. When you eat something, the taste buds give the nerves information. The nerves tell your brain what you have eaten. Then, your brain tells you what the taste is!

During Reading

- What part of your tongue does the tasting?
- What are the four tastes?

But did you know that you need something else to be able to taste? Your nose! You need to be able to smell to tell the flavor of a food. So, if you don't like how something tastes, just hold your nose. That might help you not taste it!

After Reading

- What does your tongue do?
- What does something salty taste like?

The four different tastes are sour, salty, sweet, and bitter. But your taste buds don't react differently to the four tastes. This makes some people think that we learn to taste sour, salty, sweet, and bitter.

Which taste does your tongue like best?

Vocabulary

bitter: a very unpleasant taste

papillae: something small that sticks out of your tongue and holds a group of taste buds

sour: a sharp or tart taste, like that of a lemon

Classify/Categorize

When you classify things, you put them in groups by how they are alike. In "Can You Taste That?" you read about the four different tastes—sour, salty, sweet, and bitter. Put the foods from the list in the right spot in the chart.

Foods:

cookies

lemons

bananas

pretzels

uncooked potatoes

crackers

grapefruit

Sweet: tasting like sugar	Sour: a tart taste
Salty: tasting like salt	**Bitter: unpleasant taste**

© *Teacher Created Materials*

Use Text Organizers

Section headings can tell you what a section of an article is about. How would you write section headings for the story "Can You Taste That?" to help other readers? Below are three sections of the story. Write a heading for each section.

Heading 1: _____

Taste buds on your tongue are in groups called papillae. These groups are connected to nerves. When you eat something, the taste buds give the nerves information. The nerves tell your brain what you have eaten. Then, your brain tells you what the taste is!

Heading 2: _____

But did you know that you need something else to be able to taste? Your nose! You need to be able to smell to tell the flavor of a food. So, if you don't like how something tastes, just hold your nose. That might help you not taste it!

Heading 3: _____

The four different tastes are sour, salty, sweet, and bitter. But your taste buds don't react differently to the four tastes. This makes some people think that we learn to taste sour, salty, sweet, and bitter.

Comprehension Practice

Circle the letter of the best answer.

1. What are **papillae**?
   A. large tongues
   B. the four senses
   C. groups of taste buds
   D. bitter-tasting food

2. What tells your brain you have eaten something?
   A. ears
   B. nerves
   C. eyes
   D. teeth

3. What sense other than taste is needed to tell flavor?
   A. sense of touch
   B. sense of sound
   C. sense of sight
   D. sense of smell

4. Which is not one of the four tastes?
   A. bitter
   B. sweet
   C. cold
   D. salty

5. Which of these does NOT help us taste things?
   A. nose
   B. tongue
   C. brain
   D. fingers

6. Groups of taste buds called **papillae** are connected to what?
   A. other papillae
   B. nose
   C. nerves
   D. skin

7. Which two tastes describe lemonade?
   A. sweet and sour
   B. sweet and salty
   C. sour and bitter
   D. bitter and salty

8. What would be the best title for the section that tells about smell and tastes?
   A. The Five Different Tastes
   B. Salty Things
   C. My Nose Helps Me Taste
   D. Taste Buds

© Teacher Created Materials

Transportation

Before Reading

- What are some ways people get around?
- Why do people need to go to different places?

During Reading

- What would you use to get from one country to another?
- What do people use to cross water?

After Reading

- What type of transportation do you see people using the most?
- What are other ways people can get around?

Vocabulary

travel: to visit places, to take a trip

freight: goods that are being transported

There are many different ways to get around. Many people drive cars. Other people walk. Some people ride their bikes. People always have to go places. Let's think of other ways to get from one place to another.

In the Air
When people have to travel very far, they can fly in an airplane. An airplane moves very fast. It can also hold a lot of people.

On the Sea
Some people get around by boats or ships. Boats and ships are able to move in water. Ships can hold hundreds of people at one time.

On the Land
Trains also help people get around. Trains can carry many things. Some trains hold people. Other trains hold freight.

People who can't walk use wheelchairs to move. A wheelchair is a special chair that has wheels on it. It rolls from one place to another.

These are all ways to get around. There are many other ways to get around too. Sometimes the best way to get around is just to walk!

Use Prior Knowledge and Make Connections

Using what you learned in the story and what you already know, think of different ways people get around. Fill in the circles with ways people get around. Start by using what you learned from the story.

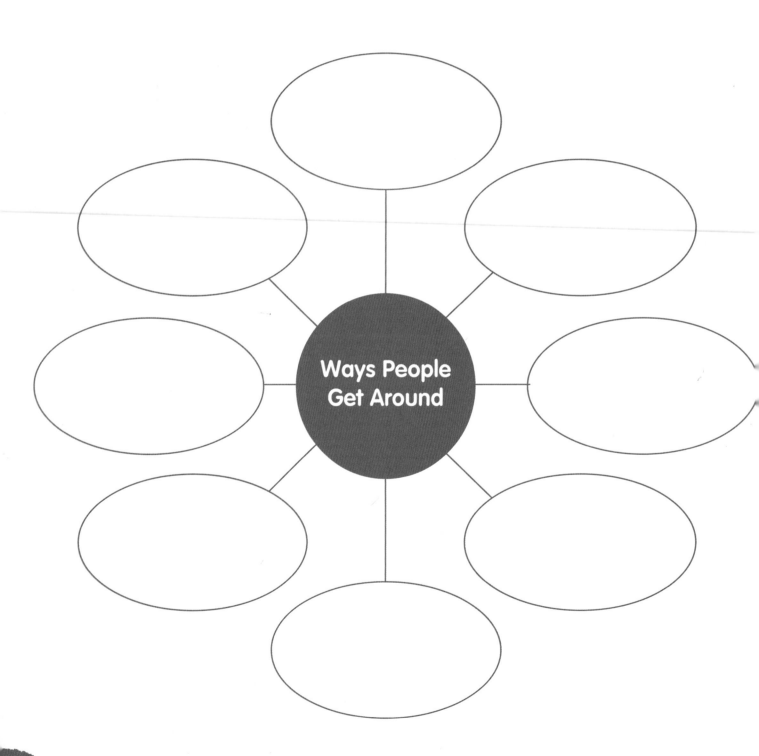

Ways People Get Around

Use Text Organizers

Section headings can tell you what a section of an article is about. Look at the three sections of the story shown below. Write the heading used in the article for each section.

Heading 1:_____

When people have to travel very far, they can fly in an airplane. An airplane moves very fast. It can also hold a lot of people.

Heading 2:_____

Some people get around by boats or ships. Boats and ships are able to move in water. Ships can hold hundreds of people at one time.

Heading 3:_____

Trains also help people get around. Trains can carry many things. Some trains hold people. Other trains hold freight.

Comprehension Practice

Circle the letter of the best answer.

1. What kind of transportation is the best for traveling on water?
   A. a car
   B. a boat or ship
   C. an airplane
   D. a train

2. What are trains used for?
   A. They are used to move many different things.
   B. They can only move people.
   C. They can only move animals.
   D. They are used to hold up traffic.

3. What do people who can't walk use to get around?
   A. roller skates
   B. skateboards
   C. wheelchairs
   D. bicycles

4. What is the best way to get around if you are visiting a neighbor?
   A. by train
   B. an airplane
   C. walking
   D. a boat or ship

5. What is another good title for this story?
   A. "Ways to Go"
   B. "My Vacation"
   C. "Wheelchairs"
   D. "Truck Drivers"

6. What is the best definition for **freight**?
   A. supplies being taken from one place to another
   B. foreign people
   C. a type of train that holds things
   D. luggage for traveling

7. If the author added more to this story, what else could be included under "On the Land"?
   A. Hot-air balloons are a fun way to travel in the air!
   B. Canoes can hold two or three people.
   C. In the military, submarines are a great way to stay safe in the water.
   D. Buses provided convenient ways to get around in cities.

8. What would a girl who lives a block away from school most likely do?
   A. walk to school
   B. take a train to school
   C. fly in an airplane to school
   D. make her little brother pull her in a wagon

   © Teacher Created Materials

The Castle

Before Reading

- What is a castle?
- What is a hike?

During Reading

- Why did James decide to hike to the castle?
- What did he find when he got to the castle?

After Reading

- How did James free the dragon?
- Are dragons real or make-believe?

Every day on his way to school, James noticed a castle up on a hill. It seemed very far away. He became curious about the castle, so one day he grabbed his walking stick and set out to explore it.

It was a long hike. He crossed streams and climbed steep hills. When James reached the castle, he knocked on the door. "Please help me!" a tiny voice begged from inside. "I'm stuck." He opened the door and peeked in.

James looked around the large room. He noticed a staircase. Halfway up the staircase there was a dragon. His foot was stuck between the rails of the banister! James ran up the stairs to help the dragon. He placed his walking stick between the railings. He pulled hard and twisted the rails apart. The dragon's foot was free!

From that day on, James and the dragon were the best of friends. James visited his new friend often. The castle never again seemed far away.

Vocabulary

curious: wanting to know more about something

banister: the handrail on a staircase

rails: the bars that hold up a banister

steep: having a sharp slope

Analyze Plot Structure

After reading "The Castle," complete the chart below. Tell what happened in the beginning, in the middle, and at the end of the story.

What happened in the beginning of the story?

What happened in the middle of the story?

How did the story end?

Analyze Characters

As you read "The Castle," look for clues in the story that tell you what the main character is like. Use what the author tells you about the character to complete the chart.

1. Who is James?

_____

_____

_____

2. Is James a real or make-believe person?

_____

3. Which words below describe James's personality? Circle all the words that tell what James is like.

selfish   curious   kind   lazy   mean   helpful

4. Tell about something James did in the story that gives us a clue about his personality.

_____

_____

_____

5. How do James's personality traits affect how the story ends?

_____

_____

_____

Comprehension Practice

Circle the letter of the best answer.

1. What kind of story is "The Castle"?
   A. real
   B. scary
   C. nonfiction
   D. make-believe

2. Where does the dragon live?
   A. in a cave
   B. in a school
   C. in a castle
   D. in a tree

3. Why was the dragon calling for help?
   A. His house was on fire.
   B. His foot was caught in a railing.
   C. He got lost in the woods.
   D. He was scared of James.

4. What was used to free the dragon?
   A. a walking stick
   B. a hose
   C. a flashlight
   D. a handrail

5. This is a story about _____.
   A. learning new things by being curious
   B. making friends
   C. being brave
   D. all of the above

6. Where would you expect to see a **banister**?
   A. around a playground
   B. on a steep hill
   C. beside a staircase
   D. in a dragon's house

7. What seemed different about the castle at the end of the story?
   A. It was a different color.
   B. It seemed smaller.
   C. The hills were not steep anymore.
   D. The castle did not seem so far away.

8. Why did the dragon become friends with James?
   A. because James was smart
   B. because he wanted James' walking stick
   C. because James helped him
   D. because there were no other dragons around

Amazing Reptiles

Have you ever wondered what it would be like to be a reptile? If you were a reptile, you would most likely hatch from an egg. You would be covered with scales. In the morning, you would be cold and move slowly. To warm up, you would lie in the sun. Then you would move quickly to find food.

If you were a reptile, you might be a crocodile, a turtle, a lizard, or a snake.

If you were a crocodile, you would have eyes on the top of your head and live in a swamp. If you were a turtle, you would have no teeth and carry your home on your back. If you were a snake, you would not have any feet. You would live in all kinds of places. If you were a lizard, you might be a chameleon. You could change the color of your skin and live in a rain forest.

Being a reptile might be fun! What kind of reptile would you like to be?

Before Reading

- What kinds of reptiles have you seen?
- Where do reptiles live?

During Reading

- What are the four main kinds of reptiles?
- In what ways are all reptiles alike?

Vocabulary

reptile: a cold-blooded, scaly animal that breathes with lungs

swamp: a low area of land that is covered with shallow water

rain forest: a thick forest that gets lots of rain

After Reading

- Where do snakes live?
- What kind of reptile carries its home on its back?

Lizard

Snake

Crocodile

Turtle

© Teacher Created Materials

Compare and Contrast

As you read, compare and contrast the different kinds of reptiles in "Amazing Reptiles." Use what you read to complete the chart.

Reptiles	How are they alike?	How are they different?
1. turtle and crocodile		
2. snake and lizard		
3. lizard and crocodile		
4. snake and turtle		

Identify Main Idea and Supporting Details

As you read "Amazing Reptiles," think about what the main idea of the selection is. Then look for small pieces of information that tell more about the main idea. Write the main idea of the selection in the large box. Write supporting details that tell more about the main idea in the small boxes.

What is the main idea of "Amazing Reptiles"?

_____

_____

Detail:

_____

Detail:

_____

Detail:

_____

Detail:

_____

Detail:

_____

Comprehension Practice

Circle the letter of the best answer.

1. What is "Amazing Reptiles" about?
    A. lizards from around the world
    B. reptiles, cold-blooded, scaly animals
    C. animals that hatch from eggs
    D. dinosaurs that lived long ago

2. Which animal is a reptile?
    A. cat
    B. spider
    C. whale
    D. snake

3. How is a snake different from a turtle?
    A. A snake moves slowly when it is cold.
    B. A snake may hatch from an egg.
    C. A snake has no feet.
    D. A snake is a reptile.

4. What is a chameleon?
    A. a type of snake
    B. a type of lizard
    C. a type of turtle
    D. a type of crocodile

5. Which is NOT true about reptiles?
    A. They have scales.
    B. Most hatch from eggs.
    C. They are cold-blooded.
    D. They are covered with fur.

6. What is a **swamp** like?
    A. dry
    B. covered with trees
    C. covered with sand
    D. very wet

7. All reptiles move slowly _____.
    A. when they are cold
    B. when they lie in the sun
    C. to catch food
    D. always

8. Which reptile has eyes on top of its head?
    A. a crocodile
    B. a turtle
    C. a snake
    D. a chameleon

© *Teacher Created Materials*

Pencil Problems

Before Reading

- Do you have a best friend?
- Have you ever gotten into a fight with him or her?

During Reading

- Why do Ming and Sarah get into a fight?
- How do they solve their problem?

After Reading

- What should Sarah and Ming have done differently?
- Who helps you with your problems?

Vocabulary

accidents: things that happen without being planned

careless: not being careful with something

ignored: did not pay attention to someone

Ming and Sarah are best friends. They spend all of their time together. The girls have been friends for two whole years. They never got into a fight, not until that day.

"Ming, can I borrow your new pencil?" Sarah asked. Ming's dad had just given her a special pencil. It was pink with hearts on it with a heart-shaped eraser.

"Of course, you're my best friend, right?" answered Ming.

Sarah used the pencil for the afternoon. As they were walking home, Ming asked for it back. Sarah looked, but she could not find it!

Ming was so upset that she ran home and cried. She was mad at Sarah for being so careless, and she wondered if her dad would be mad too.

The next day at school Sarah and Ming ignored each other. When Ming got home, her dad noticed the big frown on her face.

Ming told him what happened. Her dad said that he wasn't mad and she shouldn't be either! Sometimes accidents happen, even between best friends.

Ming realized she had been silly. She would talk to Sarah tomorrow.

Predict

When you read, you think about what might happen next. When you do this, you **predict**. Answer the following questions about "Pencil Problems."

1. At the beginning of the story, you are told that Ming and Sarah get into a fight. What did you think the fight was going to be about?

   _____

   _____

2. Did you think Ming and Sarah would talk the next day?

   _____

   _____

3. What did happen the next day at school?

   _____

   _____

4. What did you think Ming's dad was going to tell her?

   _____

   _____

5. The story does not tell if Ming and Sarah became friends again. What do you predict happened?

   _____

   _____

#50089 Reading Comprehension—Level D
© Teacher Created Materials

Analyze Plot Structure

A plot is a group of events in a story. Sometimes plots are about problems and solutions. A solution is a way a problem is solved, or the way a problem is fixed. Fill in the chart about the plot of the story "Pencil Problems."

The Plot	
1. The problem of the story:	
2. Who causes the problem:	
3. How the problem is solved:	
4. How you would have solved the problem if you were Sarah:	

Comprehension Practice

Circle the letter of the best answer.

1. Who is this story about?
   A. Sarah and Tracy
   B. Ming and Sarah
   C. Ming's dad
   D. Sarah's dad

2. Who gave Ming the pencil?
   A. Sarah
   B. her teacher
   C. her sister
   D. her dad

3. What did Ming do when she learned her pencil was lost?
   A. ran home
   B. hugged Sarah
   C. found it
   D. smiled

4. What did Sarah and Ming do the next day at school?
   A. They talked to each other.
   B. They played a game.
   C. They did not talk to each other.
   D. They found the pencil.

5. What is the main point of this story?
   A. Friends are more important than things like pencils.
   B. It is not a good idea to let your friend borrow things.
   C. Don't take your best pencil to school.
   D. A pink pencil is better than a yellow one.

6. What is an example of an **accident**?
   A. She had other pencils.
   B. The pencil wasn't very nice anyway.
   C. She looked funny when she was mad.
   D. Sarah lost the pencil.

7. When do you think Ming and Sarah will be friends again?
   A. in a week or so
   B. never
   C. the next day when Ming talks to Sarah
   D. when Ming gets a new pencil

8. What did Ming decide to do after talking to her dad?
   A. She would ignore Sarah.
   B. She would get a new pencil.
   C. She would give Sarah a pencil.
   D. She would talk to Sarah the next day.

© Teacher Created Materials

Working Dogs

Have you seen big dogs in stores or restaurants and wondered why they were there? Those dogs might have been guide dogs.

Who Uses Them?

People who are blind sometimes use guide dogs called seeing-eye dogs. These special dogs help people get around. They help them do everyday things. Some people who have hearing problems have hearing-ear dogs. These dogs tell their owners when an alarm clock goes off or when the doorbell rings.

What Do They Know?

Guide dogs learn to wear something on their backs called a harness. Their owner holds onto it. The dogs learn what words such as "left" and "right" mean. They learn to never take their owner into traffic.

How Do They Know It?

Each guide dog trains for months. Then, it spends one month working with its future owner. At that time, the owner and dog get to know one another and train together!

Where Can They Go?

Because guide dogs are trained, they are welcome almost anywhere. So, the next time you are out, don't be surprised if you see a dog. It might just be a guide dog!

Before Reading
- What is a guide dog?
- Have you ever seen a guide dog?

During Reading
- Who uses guide dogs?
- What do guide dogs learn to do?

After Reading
- Would you trust a dog to lead you around?
- What else do you think guide dogs can learn to do?

Vocabulary

blind: unable to see

harness: straps placed on an animal so the animal can pull or lead something or someone

train: to learn skills

Use Text Organizers

Headings can be helpful when you want to recall information that you have read. Read each section heading below from "Working Dogs." Then tell what information you remember from that section.

1. "Who Uses Them?"

_____

_____

_____

2. "What Do They Know?"

_____

_____

_____

3. "How Do They Know It?"

_____

_____

_____

4. "Where Can They Go?"

_____

_____

_____

#50089 Reading Comprehension—Level D   © *Teacher Created Materials*

Ask Questions

Answer the following questions about the story "Working Dogs."

1. Why do some people use guide dogs?

_____

_____

_____

_____

2. Why would people who cannot hear need a guide dog?

_____

_____

_____

_____

3. What does it take for a dog to become a guide dog?

_____

_____

_____

_____

4. Where might you see a guide dog?

_____

_____

_____

_____

Comprehension Practice

Circle the letter of the best answer.

1. Who uses guide dogs?
   A. people who want dogs to play with
   B. babies
   C. anyone who wants to
   D. people who cannot hear or cannot see

2. What special thing do guide dogs wear?
   A. a harness
   B. shoes
   C. a hat
   D. glasses

3. How long do guide dogs train?
   A. days
   B. weeks
   C. months
   D. They do not train.

4. How long do guide dogs train with their owners?
   A. two days
   B. one week
   C. one month
   D. one year

5. Why is this story called "Working Dogs?"
   A. The dogs are trained to do a job.
   B. The dogs are paid.
   C. The dogs wear a harness.
   D. The dogs hear doorbells.

6. What is the best meaning of **trained**?
   A. raised to bite people
   B. taught to do something
   C. made to look pretty
   D. bathed to smell good

7. Why might you see a dog allowed in a restaurant?
   A. It is the owner's dog.
   B. It is lost and hungry.
   C. It is working in the kitchen.
   D. It is a guide dog.

8. The section "What Do They Know" states that guide dogs learn _____.
   A. words such as "left" and "right"
   B. to keep their owner out of traffic
   C. to let their owner know when a doorbell rings
   D. All of the above

#50089 Reading Comprehension—Level D
© Teacher Created Materials

Friends for Peachy

Before Reading

- What do you do when you want to play with a friend?
- How do you feel when you can't find a friend to be with?

During Reading

- Why does Peachy Dog decide to go for a walk?
- Which friends does Peachy Dog see on her walk?

After Reading

- What does Peachy Dog find when she gets home?
- Have your friends ever surprised you?

Vocabulary

croaking: the sound a frog makes

scurry: to run quickly

celebration: a party

One sunny day, Peachy Dog decided to go for a walk and find a friend to play with. She heard her froggy friends croaking near the pond, but just as she reached the edge of the pond, all the frogs jumped into the pond. Then they were gone.

So Peachy wandered on. Suddenly, she noticed her mousy friend scurrying across a wheat field. Just as Peachy caught up to her, she disappeared down a small hole. Then she was gone.

So Peachy wandered on. She headed toward the cornfield. "Oh goody!" she thought, "It's my goosey friends!" She ran quickly toward the geese. But just as she reached them, they all spread their wings and took flight. Then they were gone.

Feeling very sad and lonely, Peachy decided to go home. Just as she pushed open the front door, she heard "Surprise!" She looked around and saw that all her friends were there, at her house. "You remembered!" she said. "You are the best friends ever!" With that, the celebration began.

Make Inferences

You can use what you already know to form ideas about what you read in "Friends for Peachy." Think about what happens in the story. Draw conclusions about things in the story to answer the questions.

1. Where do you think Peachy Dog lives?

_____

_____

_____

2. Why do you think that?

_____

_____

_____

3. Why do you think Peachy Dog's friends all ran off when they saw her coming?

_____

_____

_____

4. What kind of surprise do you think Peachy Dog's friends had planned for her?

_____

_____

_____

#50089 Reading Comprehension—Level D   © *Teacher Created Materials*

Identify Story Elements

The story "Friends for Peachy" has a plot, a setting, and characters. Answer the questions about the story elements.

"Friends for Peachy"

Characters

1. Who is the main character in the story?

_____

2. Who are the other characters in the story?

_____

_____

Setting

3. Where does the story take place?

_____

_____

Plot

4. What happens in the beginning of the story?

_____

5. What happens in the middle of the story?

_____

6. What happens at the end of the story?

_____

Comprehension Practice

Circle the letter of the best answer.

1. Why did Peachy Dog go for a walk?
   A. to find a place to swim
   B. to find a friend to play with
   C. to get some exercise
   D. to find a sunny day

2. Where did Peachy Dog find her goosey friends?
   A. in a cornfield
   B. in a house
   C. in a pond
   D. in a tree

3. How did Peachy Dog feel as she walked home?
   A. clever
   B. lonely
   C. tired
   D. happy

4. What happened when Peachy Dog got home?
   A. She took a nap.
   B. She got a surprise.
   C. She found something to eat.
   D. She began to cry.

5. What is another good title for this story?
   A. "The Mouse"
   B. "Frogs"
   C. "A Rainy Day"
   D. "Surprise Party"

6. "So Peachy wandered on." What does **wandered** mean?
   A. walked
   B. croaked
   C. looked
   D. scurried

7. What did Peachy find when she got home?
   A. The lights were out.
   B. She'd left the television on.
   C. The door was locked.
   D. There was a celebration.

8. Why do you think Peachy's friends all ran off?
   A. They did not like Peachy.
   B. They did not see her coming.
   C. They wanted to surprise Peachy at her party.
   D. They were mean.

© *Teacher Created Materials*

Going West to California

- What do you think the journey across America was like in the 1850s?
- Would you have liked to travel in a covered wagon? Why or why not?

Before Reading

- What are some places that are west of where you live?
- Why did people move west in the 1800s?

During Reading

- Where is the family in the story going?
- Why are they going there?

The wagons were packed. Our milk cow Bessie was tied on the back. It was time to go. It was 1851. Our family was moving west. We were leaving our hometown. Mama cried. It was hard to leave friends and family behind. Papa said we needed to go. He was taking us to a place where we could grow anything we wanted.

The journey was long and painful. At night Mama cooked over a campfire. We slept on the wagon floor. The trail was rough and bumpy. Sometimes when it rained, the wagon would get stuck in the mud. Then we would all have to get off and push.

After several months, we finally found the land that we were looking for. Papa cut down trees, and we built a house. Mama planted a garden. Soon we had the fields plowed and planted. By fall, Papa would harvest the crops and sell them in town.

Going west was a big decision—and a big adventure. But we are happy here now. And we are proud to call California our home.

Vocabulary

journey: a long trip

plow: to dig up dirt to get it ready to plant

harvest: to pick ripe fruits and vegetables

Analyze Plot Structure

What happens in the beginning, middle, and end of a story is called the plot. As you read the story "Going West to California," think about the plot. Then complete the chart below.

What happens in the beginning of the story?

What happens in the middle of the story?

What happens at the end of the story?

 #50089 Reading Comprehension—Level D   © Teacher Created Materials

Develop Vocabulary

Each time you read, you'll find words you may not know. Make a list of these words as you read and look up their meanings in a dictionary. Complete the chart below for words you do not know in "Going West to California."

Word	What I Think the Meaning Is	What the Dictionary Says the Word Means

Comprehension Practice

Circle the letter of the best answer.

1. What is the story all about?
   A. covered wagons
   B. moving west
   C. farming
   D. horses

2. How did the family travel west?
   A. on a train
   B. on horses
   C. in a wagon
   D. in an airplane

3. How long did the journey west take?
   A. several months
   B. several days
   C. a year
   D. one hour

4. How did the family feel about their new home?
   A. worried
   B. excited
   C. scared
   D. proud

5. Which do you think describes the family's journey?
   A. easy
   B. long
   C. short
   D. fun

6. Like most fields, why was the field in California **plowed**?
   A. so crops could be planted and grown
   B. to see if there was treasure under the ground
   C. to hide the family's money
   D. for fun

7. What did the family do when the wagon got stuck?
   A. They waited for a tow truck to come pull it out.
   B. They cried and did nothing.
   C. They yelled at the horses.
   D. They all got out and pushed the wagon.

8. What happened after the family got to California?
   A. The family opened a general store.
   B. They built a house and planted things.
   C. The wagon got stuck again.
   D. They went to meet all of their neighbors.

Changes

Katie and Betty were sisters. They lived at home with their mom and dad. Katie loved her family, but she felt different. Everyone else in her family was a butterfly and had wings. She was a caterpillar. She did not have wings. She could not fly. She felt ugly.

One day Katie was crying. Betty asked her, "What is wrong?"

Katie said, "I want to be a butterfly! I want wings. I want to fly. I want to be like you and Mom and Dad."

Betty told her, "You will be a butterfly after you change. First you will create a cocoon. You will live in it while your body changes."

Katie was scared. Betty saw that her sister was going to cry. "Katie, I haven't told you the best part. When you come out of the cocoon, you will be a beautiful butterfly!"

Katie's face lit up and she smiled. She loved being a caterpillar because she knew that one day she would be a beautiful butterfly just like Betty.

It made Betty smile to see her sister so happy.

Before Reading

- What is a caterpillar?
- What is a butterfly?

During Reading

- Why doesn't Katie want to be a caterpillar?
- Where does a caterpillar live to change into a butterfly?

After Reading

- Is Katie still upset at the end of the story? Why or why not?
- How could you make someone who is upset feel better?

Vocabulary

cocoon: a covering that keeps a caterpillar safe so it can turn into a butterfly

create: to make

Compare and Contrast

Complete the following chart, comparing and contrasting Katie and Betty from "Changes."

Katie	Betty
1. Katie is a caterpillar.	**1.**
2.	**2.** Betty looked like the rest of their family.
3.	**3.** Betty was beautiful.
4. At the end of the story, Katie was happy.	**4.**
5.	**5.** Betty had wings.
6. Katie still has changes to go through.	**6.**

     © *Teacher Created Materials*

Identify Sequence

When something has to be done in a certain order to get the final product, it is called a **process**. Put the steps in order to show how Katie from the story "Changes" will one day change.

Katie will create a cocoon.

Katie is a caterpillar.

Katie will be a beautiful butterfly.

Katie will live in the cocoon.

Katie will come out of the cocoon after her body changes.

1. Now:

_____

2. The first step for her to change:

_____

_____

3. The second step for her to change:

_____

_____

4. The last step for her to change:

_____

_____

5. In the end:

_____

_____

Comprehension Practice

Circle the letter of the best answer.

1. Why was Katie crying?
   A. She was hurt.
   B. Betty called her a name.
   C. She got into trouble.
   D. She was the only caterpillar in the family.

2. Who is Betty?
   A. Katie's friend
   B. Katie's sister
   C. Katie's mom
   D. another caterpillar

3. How did Betty make Katie feel better?
   A. She gave her a hug.
   B. She made her a cake.
   C. She told her that one day she will change into a butterfly.
   D. She showed her other caterpillars.

4. What will Katie be after she changes?
   A. a caterpillar
   B. a butterfly
   C. a firefly
   D. an ant

5. Why does Katie love being a caterpillar after Betty talks to her?
   A. She has more legs than Betty.
   B. She likes being green.
   C. She likes eating leaves.
   D. She knows she will become beautiful like Betty.

6. What is a **cocoon**?
   A. a place where a caterpillar changes into a butterfly
   B. a playground for insects
   C. a type of snack
   D. a plant

7. What was different about Katie from the rest of her family?
   A. She could not talk.
   B. She was smaller.
   C. She did not have wings.
   D. She lived in a different place.

8. What is the first stage in Katie's life?
   A. She is a beautiful butterfly.
   B. She is a cocoon.
   C. She is a moth.
   D. She is a caterpillar.

Alligator or Crocodile?

Can you tell the difference between an alligator and a crocodile?

Alligators and crocodiles use strong legs to walk on the ground. They both have short legs. Both animals are big reptiles.

Alligator

Crocodile

Both are good swimmers. They use their tails to move in the water. They do this by moving their tails from side to side to swim through the water.

Both have tough skin. They have sharp teeth and eat meat. They sleep during the day and hunt at night.

How are they different from each other? Alligators are longer than crocodiles. They also have more teeth. Look at their noses. The alligator has a short nose. It is shaped like the letter U. The crocodile has a long nose. Its nose is shaped like the letter V.

Many alligators are black. Crocodiles are brown. Animals can look the same but be very different. What other animals look the same to you? Are they really though?

Before Reading

- What is an alligator?
- What is a crocodile?

During Reading

- How are alligators and crocodiles the same?
- How are alligators and crocodiles different?

After Reading

- Are animals that look like each other always the same?
- What other animals look the same but are different?

Vocabulary

snout: the part of an animal's head that has the nose, mouth, and jaws

tough: hard to tear or cut

Compare and Contrast

When you read stories, you will find that many characters or things are the same in many ways and different in many ways. On the following chart, compare alligators and crocodiles.

Alligators and Crocodiles

Same	Different

Identify Main Idea and Supporting Details

Read "Alligator or Crocodile?" The first paragraph tells you the topic of the story. Each paragraph has a main idea. Sometimes the main idea is stated. Sometimes the main idea is not stated. Then you have to infer the main idea. Write the main idea of the paragraphs in the right-hand columns of the chart.

Main Idea Paragraph 2:	
Main Idea Paragraph 3:	
Main Idea Paragraph 4:	
Main Idea Paragraph 5:	
Main Idea Paragraph 6:	

Comprehension Practice

Circle the letter of the best answer.

1. Alligators and crocodiles are the same animal.
    A. True
    B. False

2. Alligators and crocodiles do not like the water.
    A. True
    B. False

3. Alligators have a short nose that is shaped like the letter U.
    A. True
    B. False

4. Both animals sleep during the day and hunt at night.
    A. True
    B. False

5. Crocodiles and alligators are both what?
    A. big reptiles
    B. mammals
    C. snakes
    D. good dancers

6. If I described a **snout**, what would I be talking about?
    A. a type of food
    B. a part of the head
    C. a kind of shelter
    D. a bad dream

7. Which of these things is different between alligators and crocodiles?
    A. what they eat
    B. when they hunt
    C. shape of nose
    D. how they swim

8. Why don't crocodiles and alligators get cuts easily?
    A. They are reptiles.
    B. They live in the water.
    C. They have short legs.
    D. They have tough skin.

The Big Day

My dog Plum and I are so excited! She is going to be in a dog show today, and I have to help her look her best.

First, I am going to give her a haircut, which she doesn't like at all. The sound of the electric razor scares her, and she always tries to jump off the table!

After the haircut, she gets a bath. I use a special shampoo just for dogs that makes her coat look shiny and healthy. A healthy, shiny coat is very important to the judges.

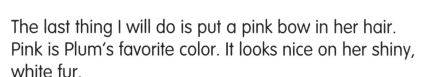

Before Reading

- What is a dog show?
- What do dogs do at a dog show?

Next, I clip her toenails, which she really doesn't like. Her nails have to be very short. She loses points if her toenails click on the floor.

During Reading

- Why are Plum and the author excited?
- What does the author do to help Plum look her best?

The last thing I will do is put a pink bow in her hair. Pink is Plum's favorite color. It looks nice on her shiny, white fur.

I bet she will be the prettiest dog in the show. Maybe she will even win a blue ribbon!

After Reading

- Why do Plum's toenails need to be clipped?
- Do you think Plum likes getting ready for the dog show?

Vocabulary

razor: a tool used to cut hair or animal fur

coat: an animal's fur

judges: people who decide which dogs win a ribbon

Identify Cause and Effect

The chart below tells about things that happen in "The Big Day." What happens is called the **effect**. Why it happens is called the **cause**. Complete the chart by telling the cause, or why each thing happens.

What Happens (Effect)	Why It Happens (Cause)
1. Plum and the author get excited.	
2. Plum has a bath and gets her fur and toenails clipped.	
3. Plum's coat looks shiny and healthy.	
4. Plum gets scared and tries to jump off the table.	

© Teacher Created Materials

Identify Sequence

As you read "The Big Day," think about the steps the author takes to get Plum ready for the dog show. Look for clue words like **first**, **after**, **next**, and **last** to help you put the steps in order and complete the chart. This order is called a sequence.

Getting Ready for the Dog Show

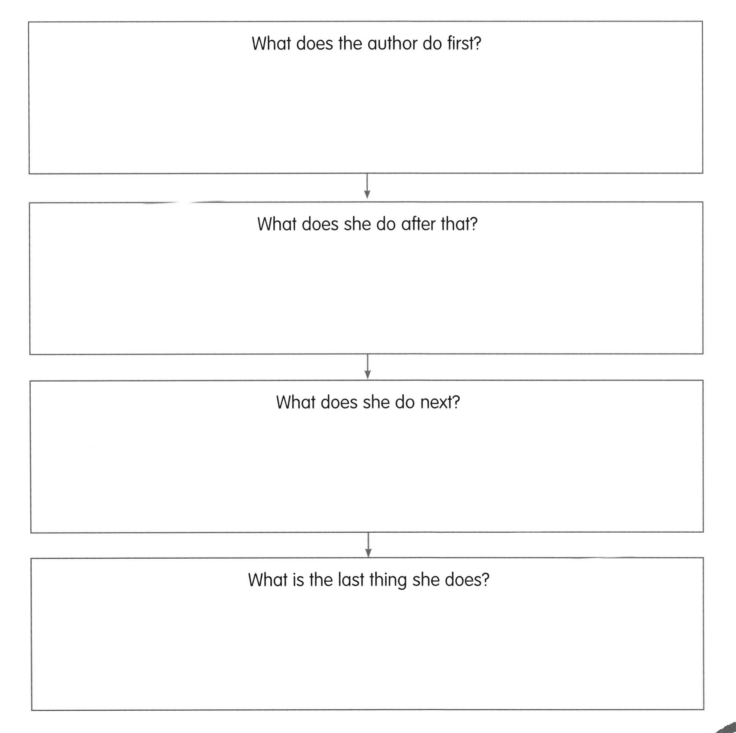

What does the author do first?

What does she do after that?

What does she do next?

What is the last thing she does?

Comprehension Practice

Circle the letter of the best answer.

1. What is Plum?
   A. a girl
   B. a dog
   C. a judge
   D. a cat

2. What is Plum scared of?
   A. water
   B. the judges
   C. cats
   D. the electric razor

3. What will happen if Plum's toenails click on the floor?
   A. She will not win.
   B. She will have to go home.
   C. She will lose points.
   D. She will win.

4. What does the author hope Plum will win?
   A. a blue ribbon
   B. a trip to Mexico
   C. a new doghouse
   D. a puppy

5. This story is mainly about _____.
   A. how to cut a dog's toenails
   B. the best shampoo for your dog
   C. why the dog is named Plum
   D. getting Plum ready for a dog show

6. Which of the following meanings of **coat** does NOT make sense in this story?
   A. Shampoo will make her coat shiny.
   B. I must wear my coat today.
   C. The judges look at her coat.
   D. Her coat will be easy to comb.

7. What is the last thing the author does to get Plum ready for the show?
   A. gives her a haircut
   B. gives her a bath
   C. clips her toenails
   D. puts a pink bow in her hair

8. Why does Plum try to jump off the table?
   A. She is bored.
   B. She is scared of the razor.
   C. She wants to chase a cat.
   D. The table is cold.

A Little Bit of Sand

Have you ever seen a pearl or a whole necklace made of pearls? You should know how hard it was for each of those pearls to be made!

Pearls form in special kinds of oysters. An oyster is a sea animal that lives in a shell, or a shellfish. The inside of an oyster's shell is lined with nacre. This lining is also called the pearly layer. It is very shiny, like a pearl.

Sand or some other small things get into an oyster. When the sand is covered again and again with nacre, a pearl forms! People find the oysters and take the pearls. The pearls are used as jewelry.

Only some kinds of oysters create beautiful and shiny pearls. Most of these oysters live in tropical seas.

Not all pearls are round. They can come in many strange shapes. But when people make jewelry with pearls, they want them round.

Today, making pearls is not left up to nature. Trained workers put a piece of nacre into oyster shells. Then they put the oysters into cages in the ocean. Then pearls form. In some oysters it can take almost three years for a pearl to form!

Before Reading

- What is a pearl?
- Where do pearls come from?

During Reading

- What is nacre?
- How can people help make pearls?

After Reading

- Where are most pearl oysters found?
- Why do many people wear pearls?

Vocabulary

nacre: also called mother-of-pearl, hard shiny layer on the inside of some shells

oyster: a shellfish

pearl: a round, shiny gem made inside an oyster

tropical: of Earth's middle region

Identify Sequence

In the story "A Little Bit of Sand," you learn how a pearl is formed. The steps are listed below. As you read the story, think about the order of the steps. Write the steps in the correct order.

People find the oysters and take the pearls.

The sand is covered again and again with nacre.

A pearl forms!

Sand or some other small things get into an oyster.

The pearls are used as jewelry.

Step 1:	
Step 2:	
Step 3:	
Step 4:	
Step 5:	

Identify Main Idea and Supporting Details

Read "A Little Bit of Sand." What is the main idea of the article? What details tell more about the main idea? Write the main idea of the selection in the chart. Then, write the supporting details in the chart.

Main Idea:
Supporting Detail 1:
Supporting Detail 2:
Supporting Detail 3:
Supporting Detail 4:

Comprehension Practice

Circle the letter of the best answer.

1. This article tells how _____ are made.
   A. oysters
   B. pearls
   C. shells
   D. fish

2. An oyster is a type of _____.
   A. gem
   B. whale
   C. shellfish
   D. boat

3. _____ gets inside of oysters to make pearls form.
   A. water
   B. seaweed
   C. sand
   D. sunlight

4. People use pearls for _____.
   A. toys
   B. jewelry
   C. food
   D. candy

5. What main point does the author make about making pearls?
   A. It is very easy to do.
   B. A few are made each week.
   C. Nobody likes pearls anymore.
   D. It can take up to three years.

6. What does **nacre** become?
   A. a pile of sand
   B. a pearl
   C. a shell
   D. a butterfly

7. Where do most of the oysters that make beautiful pearls live?
   A. near the North Pole
   B. in tropical seas
   C. in jewelry stores
   D. in lakes

8. What is the first thing workers do to make pearls?
   A. put a piece of nacre in the oyster shells
   B. wait three years
   C. put the oysters in cages
   D. make the pearls round

#50089 Reading Comprehension—Level D © *Teacher Created Materials*

Game Time

Speed skaters

Have you ever watched the Olympic Games? If you have, then you have seen the best athletes in the world compete.

The games started in Greece long, long ago. They were not played for a long time. Then in 1896, the Summer Games were started again. The Winter Games did not start until 1924.

At first, the Summer and Winter Games were held in the same year every four years. In 1994, the Winter and Summer Games were split up. Now, every two years games are held. One year it's the Summer Games. Two years later it's the Winter Games. So, each set of games are held every four years. They are just on different schedules!

The games have a symbol. It is known all over the world. It is five linked rings. The rings are blue, yellow, black, green, and red. Each ring stands for a continent.

In the Winter Games, you can see hockey, skating, skiing, and other sports. In the Summer Games, you can see baseball, swimming, track, and more!

Which sport would you like to play?

Before Reading

- What Olympic sport do you watch?
- Do you know where Olympic Games have been held?

During Reading

- Where were the very first Olympic Games held?
- When were the Winter Games started?

After Reading

- When are the Olympics held?
- What are some summer and winter Olympic sports?

Vocabulary

compete: to take part in a sporting event

linked: joined together

symbol: something that stands for something else

Identify Author's Purpose and Viewpoint

Authors write for many different reasons. Think about why the author wrote "Game Time." Then answer the questions.

1. What is the subject of the story?

_____

2. Does this story mostly entertain?

_____

3. Does this story tell facts about the subject? If so, write three facts given in the article.

_____

_____

_____

_____

4. Does the story try to persuade you to do something? If so, tell what the story tries to get you to do.

_____

_____

5. Does the story try to persuade you to believe something? If so, tell what the story tries to get you to believe.

_____

_____

_____

6. Think about your answers to questions 1–5. Then circle the reason why the author wrote the article.

    to entertain
    to inform
    to persuade

 © Teacher Created Materials

Use Prior Knowledge and Make Connections

Using what you learned in the story and what you already know, think of different sports that are played in the Olympics. Fill in the circles with the Olympic events. Start by naming the sports from the story.

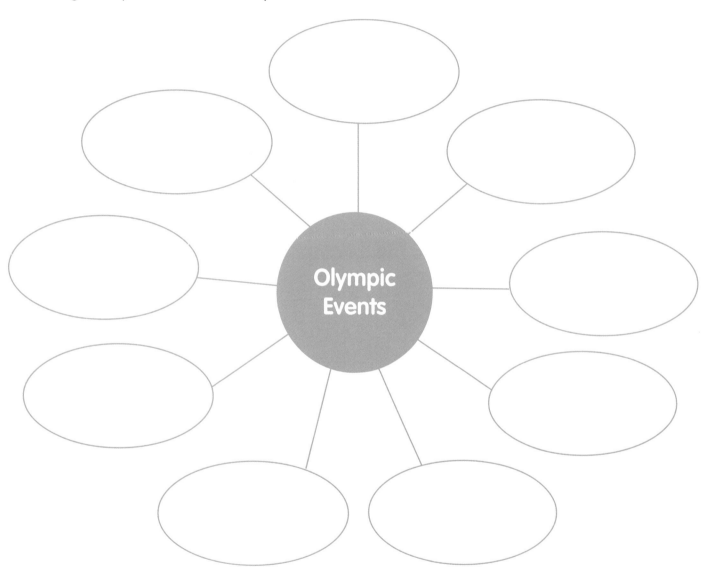

Comprehension Practice

Circle the letter of the best answer.

1. Where were the very first Olympic Games played?
   - **A.** China
   - **B.** the United States
   - **C.** France
   - **D.** Greece

2. In what year were the Olympic Games started again?
   - **A.** 1722
   - **B.** 1896
   - **C.** 1920
   - **D.** 1980

3. How often do we have an Olympics today?
   - **A.** every year
   - **B.** every two years
   - **C.** every five years
   - **D.** every eight years

4. How many rings does the Olympics symbol have?
   - **A.** two
   - **B.** three
   - **C.** four
   - **D.** five

5. What is the main idea of this story?
   - **A.** It tells about ice skating.
   - **B.** It tells many facts about the Olympic Games.
   - **C.** It is supposed to make me laugh.
   - **D.** It is about baseball and swimming.

6. Which of the following is an example of a **symbol**?
   - **A.** a sport
   - **B.** one of the five founders of the Olympic games
   - **C.** the five linked rings of the Olympic sign
   - **D.** a flavor of ice cream

7. What is the author's purpose in writing this story?
   - **A.** to inform the reader
   - **B.** to make the reader laugh
   - **C.** to persuade the reader
   - **D.** to amuse the reader

8. Which sport would you NOT see in the Winter Olympics?
   - **A.** ice skating
   - **B.** skiing
   - **C.** ice hockey
   - **D.** swimming

 #50089 Reading Comprehension—Level D   © *Teacher Created Materials*

Mac Makes a Difference

Before Reading

- At what outdoor place do you like to spend time?
- What does it mean to litter?

During Reading

- Where does Mac like to spend his time?
- How does he help the environment?

After Reading

- What did Mac see that made him so upset?
- How do you try to help the environment?

Mac has always loved going to the beach. He spends as much time there as he can.

Today after school, Mac and his mom grabbed their beach gear and headed to the shore. It was a bright, sunny day.

The beach was full by the time they got there. It seemed like everyone had the same idea today. When they found a spot, Mac sat down and began to relax.

Soon Mac noticed something strange. There was an empty water bottle in the sand. Then, a paper bag was blowing down by the water. People had littered all over the beach!

Mac was mad. His mom explained that a lot of people litter instead of using garbage cans. If Mac wanted it to stop, he would have to work to save the beach.

He worked hard. Mac got a group to help clean up. He put up signs saying "No Littering" and got his town to add more garbage cans in the area. Most of all, he let people know how bad littering is for the environment.

Mac worked hard to make a difference!

Vocabulary

environment: the natural world of plants and animals

gear: clothes and other equipment needed for an activity

littering: making a place dirty by throwing trash on the ground

Identify Story Elements

The story "Mac Makes a Difference" has a plot, a setting, and characters. Answer the questions to describe these story elements.

Characters

1. Who is the main character in the story?

_____

2. Who are the other characters in the story?

_____

_____

Setting

3. Where does the story take place?

_____

_____

Plot

4. What happens in the beginning of the story?

_____

5. What happens in the middle of the story?

_____

6. What happens at the end of the story?

_____

     © Teacher Created Materials

Analyze Characters

As you read "Mac Makes a Difference," look for clues in the story that tell you what the characters are like. Use what the author tells you about the characters to answer the questions.

1. What do you know about Mac?

_____

_____

_____

_____

2. Which words below describe Mac's personality? Circle all the words that tell what Mac is like.

mean   caring   lazy   hardworking   kind

3. What did Mac do in the story that helped you learn about his personality?

_____

_____

_____

4. How do Mac's personality traits affect how the story ends?

_____

_____

_____

Comprehension Practice

Circle the letter of the best answer.

1. Who went to the beach with Mac?
   A. his best friend
   B. his dog
   C. his mom
   D. Mac went by himself.

2. What problem did Mac notice at the beach?
   A. It started to rain.
   B. People had littered on the beach.
   C. He lost his beach ball.
   D. The water was too cold.

3. How did Mac feel about the problem?
   A. mad
   B. sad
   C. happy
   D. did not care

4. What did the signs say that Mac put up?
   A. "No Swimming"
   B. "No Littering"
   C. "No Dancing"
   D. "No Food or Drinks"

5. As well as working hard himself, what else did Mac do?
   A. He got others to help.
   B. He took some time off.
   C. He helped his family.
   D. He stopped going to the beach.

6. If something is bad for the **environment**, that means it is bad for _____.
   A. rivers
   B. birds
   C. bushes
   D. all of the above

7. What kind of person is Mac?
   A. He is willing to work hard to fix problems.
   B. He complains about everything.
   C. He is easy-going and doesn't let things bother him.
   D. He is a bit selfish and only does things that benefit him.

8. What is one thing Mac did to save the beach from being littered?
   A. He threw all the trash he found into the sea.
   B. He ignored it and made a point of not littering himself.
   C. He told his mom to fix it.
   D. He put up signs to remind people to not litter.

The Oceans

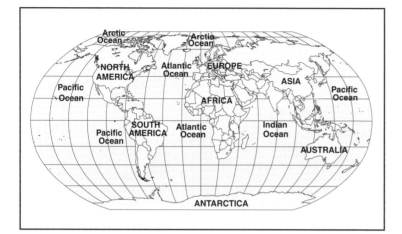

Earth has four oceans. Their names are the Atlantic, Pacific, Indian, and Arctic oceans. All four oceans touch each other. They are like one great big body of water. The Pacific Ocean is the biggest one. Some parts of an ocean are very deep. Other parts only cover your toes!

Oceans give us many things. They are filled with fish and plants. Some fish are smaller than your hand. Other fish are bigger than a car. The fish and shellfish are used for food. Some of them are used to make fish oil and food for animals. Pets eat some of the food made from ocean fish.

Oil is found deep in the ocean. Wells pump oil and gas. The ocean tides can be used to make electricity. Sand and gravel from the ocean are used for building. Ocean algae and other marine life give us sources of medicines. Oceans provide many things for us to use in our daily lives. What ocean is closest to you?

Before Reading

- What is an ocean made up of?
- What is the nearest ocean to you?

During Reading

- How many oceans are there?
- What lives in oceans?

After Reading

- Name all of the oceans in the world.
- What things do oceans give us?

Vocabulary

ocean: a body of water that covers three-fourths of Earth

shellfish: sea animals with a shell, such as crabs

tide: the rise and fall of the ocean

algae: plantlike living things found in the ocean

Summarize and Paraphrase

When you write a summary, you have to think about important information in the article. Reread the selection on oceans. Then write several sentences as a summary that tells what you have learned about oceans.

Oceans

_____

_____

_____

_____

_____

_____

_____

_____

_____

_____

_____

_____

_____

_____

_____

_____

Ask Questions

As you read, you may discover that you have questions about what you are reading. Use the following Questions and Answers chart to write the questions you have as you read. Then record the answers you find as you read.

Questions	Answers

Comprehension Practice

Circle the letter of the best answer.

1. How many oceans are there in the world?
   A. two
   B. three
   C. four
   D. six

2. Which of the following is not an ocean?
   A. Pacific
   B. Michigan
   C. Atlantic
   D. Indian

3. What can be made using ocean tides?
   A. oil
   B. cat food
   C. electricity
   D. fish oil

4. What is found in the ocean that can be used to make medicines?
   A. gas
   B. oil
   C. gravel
   D. algae

5. All four oceans are really _____.
   A. cold
   B. one big body of water
   C. made up of smaller oceans
   D. small

6. What word describes the rise and fall of oceans?
   A. Arctic
   B. tide
   C. gravity
   D. electricity

7. Which of the following is NOT a logical question to ask?
   A. What is an example of a fish that is bigger than a car?
   B. Which oceans surround Asia?
   C. Wasn't a fifth ocean just discovered on Mars?
   D. Which is the biggest ocean?

8. According to the story, which of the following live in the ocean?
   A. fish and shellfish
   B. scuba divers
   C. dogs and cats
   D. algae

    © Teacher Created Materials

The Sun

The sun is a very bright and hot star. Like all stars, it is a ball of hot gas. The sun may look small, but it is much bigger than Earth. It looks small because it is so far away. It is about 93 million miles, or 150 million kilometers, from Earth to the sun!

Before Reading

- Where is the sun?
- What does the sun do?

During Reading

- What is the sun?
- What makes day and night?

After Reading

- What would happen if we didn't have the sun?
- Did you see the sun today?

Vocabulary

Earth: the planet on which we live

star: a mass of hot gas that shines by its own light

revolve: to move around something in a circle

rotate: to spin

The sun's light and heat travel very far to reach Earth. Living things need the heat and light to grow and live. For example, plants use sunlight to make food. Then people eat some of these plants.

The sun is at the center of our solar system. Like the other planets in the system, Earth revolves around the sun. That means that it travels around the sun. It takes one year for Earth to make a complete trip. Earth is tilted as it makes this trip. This tilt makes the sunlight hit Earth differently at times during its trip around the sun. That is what causes seasons to change.

Earth also rotates as it revolves around the sun. Earth makes one complete spin each day. The part of Earth that faces the sun has day. The part of Earth that is not facing the sun has night.

The sun is a very important part of our lives. It keeps us warm and helps things around us grow. Because of it, we have day and night and our seasons. Can you imagine living without the sun?

Make Inferences

After reading the selection "The Sun," answer the question: What would the world be like if there were no sun?

Think about the things that the sun does everyday, and imagine life without the help of the sun. Write several sentences telling what the world would be like. Then draw a picture to illustrate what you wrote.

_____

_____

_____

_____

_____

_____

   © Teacher Created Materials

Use Prior Knowledge and Make Connections

Use what you learned in the story "The Sun" and what you already knew to write six sentences about the sun and why it is important.

1. _____

_____

2. _____

_____

3. _____

_____

4. _____

_____

5. _____

_____

6. _____

_____

Comprehension Practice

Circle the letter of the best answer.

1. Which planets revolve around the sun?
   A. only Earth
   B. none
   C. only Earth and Pluto
   D. all nine of them

2. Where is the sun at night when we are sleeping?
   A. The sun is on the other side of Earth.
   B. The sun is sleeping too.
   C. It finds people who aren't sleeping.
   D. The sun hides at night.

3. What does the sun do for plants?
   A. kills them
   B. nothing
   C. waters them
   D. gives light and heat

4. What would happen if there were no sun?
   A. Nothing would happen.
   B. People would be sad.
   C. It would be very hot.
   D. It would be very cold and dark.

5. Which of the following is true about the sun in our solar system?
   A. It is much bigger than Earth.
   B. It revolves around the planets.
   C. It is like any other planet.
   D. It is part of another solar system.

6. How does something that **revolves** move?
   A. back and forth
   B. in a circular way
   C. from Earth to the sun
   D. in an explosive way

7. The sun and other stars shine because they are made of _____.
   A. metal
   B. electricity
   C. hot gas
   D. hot oil

8. Without the sun, what would Earth not have?
   A. rocks
   B. trees or people
   C. a moon
   D. stars

 #50089 Reading Comprehension—Level D   © *Teacher Created Materials*

Community Helpers

Every community has people who help others. These people are called community helpers. There are many different kinds of jobs that helpers have.

Firefighters help if there is a fire. They use fire trucks. Each truck has a big ladder, which helps firefighters reach people in high places.

Firefighters must wear heavy clothes to keep the fire from burning them. They also wear helmets on their heads. That is in case things fall on them. Their job is to put out fires and save people.

Police are helpers too. They drive cars with red and blue flashing lights. Police cars make loud noises. The lights and the noise tell people they are on the way. Police help in many ways. When you call for help in an emergency, the police will always come.

Ambulance drivers are also very important. They drive to emergencies very fast. They use flashing lights and loud noises too. They take people to the hospital if they are hurt, so they can see a doctor.

All of these workers are examples of community helpers. There are many other people in your community who help too!

Before Reading

- Why is it important to know people who can help you?
- Who do you call in an emergency?

During Reading

- What are ways firefighters help people?
- What emergencies do the police help with?

After Reading

- Who are other community helpers?
- What can you do to help people?

Vocabulary

helmet: a hat that is hard and protects the head

ambulance: a vehicle used to take people to the hospital

emergency: when someone or something needs help quickly

Classify/Categorize

In the story "Community Helpers," you learned about people in your community who can help during an emergency. Not all community helpers help during emergencies. On the chart below, list people who help during emergencies, in the community, and at school. Use the community helpers listed in the box below.

Community Helpers

mail carrier	teacher	firefighter	doctor
crossing guard	principal	police officer	trash collector

Community	Emergency	School

Describe another community helper that is not mentioned in the story. Tell about his/her job.

_____

_____

_____

_____

© Teacher Created Materials

Identify Cause and Effect

Read "Community Helpers." Several causes and effects are given in the article. An **effect** is something that happens. A **cause** is the reason it happens. Complete the chart below by identifying the causes and effects.

Cause	Effect
1. Fire trucks have big ladders.	
2.	Firefighters are protected from getting burned.
3. Firefighters wear helmets.	
4.	People know that the police are on the way in an emergency.

Comprehension Practice

Circle the letter of the best answer.

1. What do community helpers do?
   A. cause trouble
   B. help other people
   C. act mean to other people
   D. give away free things

2. Why do firefighters use helmets?
   A. to keep water off them
   B. so people know they are firefighters
   C. to protect their heads
   D. so their faces do not get dirty

3. How do the police get to emergencies?
   A. They come in cars with flashing lights and sirens.
   B. They take a taxi to get there as fast as they can.
   C. Police officers don't go to emergencies.
   D. They ride on a fire truck.

4. What do ambulance drivers do when someone is hurt?
   A. They call for help.
   B. They quickly drive the person to the hospital.
   C. They do surgery on the person.
   D. They wait for the person to feel better.

5. What are examples of common community helpers?
   A. firefighters, police, and ambulance drivers
   B. people who start fires
   C. university students
   D. airplane pilots and flight attendants

6. If there is an **emergency**, what should people do?
   A. know and call a phone number to bring help quickly
   B. scream loudly until someone comes to help
   C. run away to their neighbor's house
   D. cover their eyes and hide until it's over

7. Why do fire trucks have big ladders?
   A. to help in case the truck gets stuck
   B. to help firefighters reach people in high places
   C. to help firefighters get cats out of trees
   D. to let people know that this is a fire truck

8. Other kinds of community helpers might be _____.
   A. school-crossing guards
   B. doctors and nurses
   C. trash collectors
   D. all of the above

The Spelling Bee

The final round of the spelling bee is tomorrow. Jonas, Manuel, and Kyla are the final three contestants.

Jonas isn't looking forward to it. He doesn't like spelling bees that much. He doesn't care if he wins or not. So, Jonas decides to play football rather than study.

Manuel wants to win very badly. He studies the words all night long. He has his mother quiz him several times. He even practices spelling the words backwards! Manuel wants to be prepared.

Before Reading

- What is a spelling bee?
- Have you ever been in a contest?

During Reading

- How does Jonas feel about the spelling bee?
- Why does Kyla quit studying and go to bed?

After Reading

- Who studied the hardest for the spelling bee?
- How would you feel if you were in the final round of a spelling bee?

Kyla has never been in a contest before. She feels nervous. She wants to win but is not sure she can. She tries to study, but the words are hard to spell. So, she gives up and goes to bed.

At 9:00 the next morning, the spelling bee begins. The contestants stand in front of their class. One by one, Mr. Phelps reads the words. Before long, there is a winner. The class claps and cheers for the winner.

"Congratulations!" said Mr. Phelps. "Now, it's on to the City Championship!"

Vocabulary

contestant: someone who competes in a contest

quiz: to test knowledge by asking questions

nervous: uneasy, anxious

Predict

When you read a story, you can use clues in the story to predict what happens. As you read "The Spelling Bee," look for clues to help you predict who won the spelling bee. Write your prediction below.

Predict:

Who won the spelling bee?

_____

Support Your Prediction:

What clues did you use to make your prediction?

_____

_____

_____

_____

_____

_____

_____

_____

_____

_____

Analyze Characters

The author of "The Spelling Bee" tells us what the characters in the story are like and what they think. As you read the story, look for what the author tells us about the characters in the story. Then, circle the words that describe each character and explain your choice.

Jonas

hard working   doesn't like spelling bees   likes football

_____

_____

_____

Manuel

studies hard   likes to win   nervous about being a contestant

_____

_____

_____

Kyla

believes in herself   nervous about being a contestant   never gives up

_____

_____

_____

Comprehension Practice

Circle the letter of the best answer.

1. How many contestants are in the final round of the spelling bee?
   A. three
   B. four
   C. five
   D. six

2. _____ studied very hard for the spelling bee.
   A. Jonas
   B. Manuel
   C. Kyla
   D. Mr. Phelps

3. Who thought the words for the spelling bee were hard to spell?
   A. Jonas
   B. Manuel
   C. Kyla
   D. Mr. Phelps

4. What does the winner of the spelling bee get?
   A. The winner gets an A in spelling.
   B. The winner goes to the City Championship.
   C. The winner gets an award from the principal.
   D. The winner gets a special field trip.

5. What is the purpose of a spelling bee?
   A. to make contestants nervous
   B. to get people excited about spelling
   C. to give people a way to show off
   D. to give bees something to do besides make honey

6. What is an example of being **nervous**?
   A. Someone wanting to see a movie.
   B. Not being able to decide what to wear.
   C. Being afraid you won't do well in a contest.
   D. Sneezing a lot.

7. Why does Jonas decide to play football?
   A. He doesn't really care about the spelling bee.
   B. He has a new helmet he wants to try out.
   C. The football championship is coming up.
   D. His dad tells him to play football.

8. From what the story tells us, who is most likely to win the spelling bee?
   A. Kyla, because she wants to win a trophy.
   B. Mr. Phelps, because he knows everything.
   C. Jonas, because he is not nervous at all.
   D. Manuel, because he puts the most effort into studying.

   © *Teacher Created Materials*

The Land of the Rising Sun

Imagine sailing across the ocean. If you go far enough, you would end up in Japan. Japan lies in East Asia. The sun rises in the east. So, Japan is called "the land of the rising sun." A rising sun is pictured on the Japanese flag. The flag is white with one red circle.

Japan is a small country that is made up of many islands. The four main islands are the tops of mountains. These mountains sit on the ocean floor. There are lots of volcanoes and earthquakes in Japan.

One of the biggest cities in the world, Tokyo, is in Japan. Tokyo is a very busy and crowded modern city.

Many things in Japan are different from other parts of the world. For example, the Japanese eat their food with chopsticks. Chopsticks are thin pieces of wood. They look a little like pencils. The tables are low. So, the Japanese kneel on cushions when they eat.

Visiting Japan would be fun. What would you like to do there?

Before Reading

- Where does the sun rise?
- What do you know about Japan?

During Reading

- Why is Japan called "the land of the rising sun"?
- What do people in Japan use to eat their food with?

After Reading

- How is Tokyo like other big cities?
- What other countries are in Asia?

Vocabulary

volcano: a mountain that hot lava comes out of
earthquake: the shaking of the earth
modern: up-to-date and full of new things

Compare and Contrast

As you read "The Land of the Rising Sun," think about how Japan is like your own country and how it is different from your country. Use what you read to complete the activity.

1. Name one way in which Japan and your own country are alike.

   _____

   _____

   _____

2. Name three ways in which Japan is different from your country.

   a. _____

   _____

   _____

   b. _____

   _____

   _____

   c. _____

   _____

   _____

 　　　　　　　　　　　　　© Teacher Created Materials

Visualize

Sometimes when we read, we make pictures in our minds about the things we read about. As you read "The Land of the Rising Sun," think about what things look like. Use the pictures in your mind to complete the activity.

1. Draw a picture of what you think the Japanese flag looks like.	**2.** Draw a picture of what you think Tokyo looks like.
3. Draw a picture of what you think chopsticks look like.	**4.** Draw a picture of a Japanese family eating dinner.

Comprehension Practice

Circle the letter of the best answer.

1. Where is Japan?
   A. in far East Asia
   B. in Western Europe
   C. in North America
   D. in Africa

2. What is Japan called?
   A. the land of the setting sun
   B. the land of the rising sun
   C. the island of the sun
   D. the nation of the sun

3. What is Tokyo?
   A. a country
   B. a mountain
   C. an island
   D. a city

4. What are chopsticks?
   A. a kind of Japanese food
   B. sticks used to eat with
   C. sharp sticks used to chop wood
   D. Japanese pencils

5. Why is Japan called "the land of the rising sun"?
   A. It is on an island.
   B. People in Japan all get up early in the morning.
   C. It is in East Asia and the sun rises in the east.
   D. When their volcanoes erupt, they look like the sun.

6. Tokyo is a **modern** city, so it probably has _____.
   A. many cars, buses, and big buildings
   B. only a few people and dirt roads
   C. horses, cows, and sheep
   D. a lot of Japanese restaurants

7. What does Japan's flag look like?
   A. It is white with a red circle in the middle.
   B. It is red with a white circle in the middle.
   C. It has red and white stripes and a blue circle.
   D. It is white with a red crescent moon.

8. Why is Japan different from most countries?
   A. It has a flag.
   B. It is made up of many islands.
   C. It has cities.
   D. It has people.

#50089 Reading Comprehension—Level D © *Teacher Created Materials*

What Makes an Insect an Insect

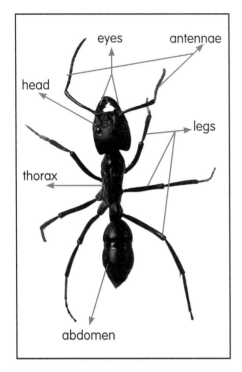

eyes, antennae, head, legs, thorax, abdomen

How are a bee, an ant, and a fly the same? For one thing, they are all insects. But why?

Well, first of all, they all have six legs and three main body parts. The body parts are the head, the thorax, and the abdomen.

An insect's head has eyes and a mouth. And many have antennae too. They are used to feel, taste, and smell things.

The middle part of an insect's body is the thorax. If an insect has wings, this is where you'll find them.

The hind part of an insect's body is the abdomen. It is usually the largest part of an insect's body. You have one of these too. Some people might call it your belly.

Insects have skeletons too. But their skeletons are on the outside of their body. They are called exoskeletons. The skeletons are very hard, so they protect the soft inside part of the insect's body.

So, next time you see a bug, look at it closely. Is it an insect or not?

Before Reading

- What is an insect?
- What kind of insects are common where you live?

During Reading

- How many legs do all insects have?
- What part of an insect's body is the largest?

After Reading

- How is an insect's skeleton different from a human skeleton?
- Is a worm an insect?

Vocabulary

hind: back, rear
skeleton: the bone structure inside bodies
antennae: the feelers on an insect's head
exoskeleton: the hard covering on the outside of bodies

Classify/Categorize

When you read "What Makes an Insect an Insect," you learned about how all insects are the same. Look carefully at the pictures below. Decide which are insects and which are not. Write each picture name in the correct column in the chart.

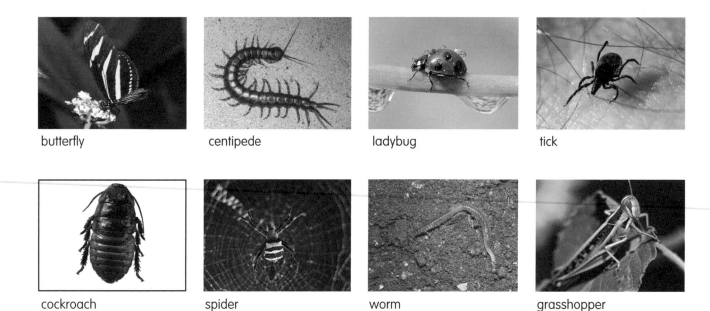

butterfly centipede ladybug tick

cockroach spider worm grasshopper

Insect	Not an Insect

© Teacher Created Materials

Develop Vocabulary

Sometimes when we read and learn new things, we learn new words too. Look for the words in the column as you read "What Makes an Insect an Insect." Choose the correct word to complete each sentence. Write the word on the line.

thorax	antennae	exoskeleton	abdomen	head	insect

1. Insects use their _____ to feel, taste, and smell things.

2. The _____ is the largest part of an insect's body.

3. A bug with eight legs and two main body sections is not an _____.

4. An insect's _____ protects its soft inner body.

5. If an insect has wings, they will be attached to its _____.

6. An insect's eyes and mouth are on its _____.

Comprehension Practice

Circle the letter of the best answer.

1. If a wasp is an insect, it will have _____ legs.
   A. two
   B. four
   C. six
   D. eight

2. How many main body parts do all insects have?
   A. one
   B. three
   C. six
   D. eight

3. What is the largest part of an insect's body called?
   A. abdomen
   B. antennae
   C. thorax
   D. head

4. How is an insect's skeleton different from a human skeleton?
   A. It has more bones in it.
   B. It is made of skin.
   C. It is on the outside of the body.
   D. It is on the inside of the body.

5. Which of the following is NOT true of insects?
   A. They may have antennae.
   B. They have wet noses.
   C. They have six legs.
   D. They have an exoskeleton.

6. Where is an **exoskeleton**?
   A. on the outside of the body
   B. on the inside of the body
   C. both outside and inside the body
   D. around a layer of soft skin

7. In which category would you find information about an insect's abdomen?
   A. the middle part of the body
   B. the head
   C. the skeleton
   D. the lower body

8. Spiders have eight legs and two main body parts. What can you infer about spiders?
   A. They cannot be insects.
   B. They are half insect, half reptile.
   C. They can run faster than insects.
   D. Two of their legs don't work.

#50089 Reading Comprehension—Level D   © *Teacher Created Materials*

All Kinds of Families

Before Reading

- What is a family?
- Who can be a part of a family?

During Reading

- How big can a family be?
- Are all families the same?

After Reading

- Who are members of your family besides the people you live with?
- Why do people have different types of families?

Who is a part of your family?

Many people live at home with their mom, dad, brothers, and sisters. Some have a lot of siblings. Other people don't have any! Families come in many sizes. They can be big or small.

Some people do not live with their mom and dad together. They might live with their mom or their dad only.

Some live with their grandma and grandpa. Others live with aunts and uncles.

A lot of people live alone. Some will call their pets their family, while others are happy being on their own.

But children always need to live with adults. Adults keep them safe, help them learn, and do many other grown-up jobs! Children can't live alone. They need to grow up first!

All families are not the same. But no matter what kind of family you have, it's made of people who care about you and each other!

Vocabulary

siblings: brothers and sisters

aunt: your mother's or father's sister, or your uncle's wife

uncle: your mother's or father's brother, or your aunt's husband

Develop Vocabulary

Read "All Kinds of Families." It names different family members. Write the name of the family member next to the description.

aunt	brother	dad	grandma
grandpa	mom	sister	uncle

1. a girl sibling _____

2. a female parent _____

3. a parent's brother _____

4. a male parent _____

5. a parent's mother _____

6. a boy sibling _____

7. a parent's father _____

8. a parent's sister _____

Identify Main Idea and Supporting Details

Think about what the main idea is as you read the story. Then, look for small pieces of information, or supporting details, that tell more about the main idea. Write the main idea and supporting details of the selection in the boxes.

Main Idea:

Supporting Detail 1:

Supporting Detail 2:

Supporting Detail 3:

Supporting Detail 4:

Comprehension Practice

Circle the letter of the best answer.

1. Which of these is a name for a sibling?
   A. pet
   B. mother
   C. uncle
   D. sister

2. What family member listed is NOT in the story?
   A. aunts
   B. uncles
   C. grandpas
   D. cousins

3. What does the story say can be called family besides people?
   A. plants
   B. cars
   C. animals
   D. toys

4. Why does the story say children can't live alone?
   A. They would get bored.
   B. They need adults to keep them safe.
   C. Children can't reach high places.
   D. Children can't get jobs.

5. What does this story tell about families?
   A. They always have a mom and a dad.
   B. They are made up of people who care about each other.
   C. They always have children in them.
   D. They need to have pets.

6. Who could my **aunt** be?
   A. my mom or dad's sister
   B. my grandma
   C. my older sister
   D. my cousin

7. Some children do not live with a mom or dad, but all children _____.
   A. have pets
   B. have a TV in their bedroom
   C. have siblings
   D. need to live with an adult

8. What is true about keeping children safe and helping them learn?
   A. They are things children can do for themselves.
   B. They are not very important.
   C. They are grown-up jobs.
   D. They are things only siblings can do.

The Ball Game

Before Reading

- What is softball?
- Have you ever played softball?

During Reading

- Is a baseball larger than a softball?
- What is the same about softball and baseball?

After Reading

- When and where did softball start?
- Would you rather be on a softball or baseball team? Why?

It might look like baseball. It might sound like baseball. But softball is not baseball. It is a different sport!

In softball, pitchers throw the ball underhand. In baseball, they throw it overhand.

A softball game has seven innings. A baseball game has nine. The softball field is smaller than a baseball field. A softball is bigger than a baseball. It is softer than a hard baseball too.

However, the two sports use the same gear. Both use a bat, ball, and gloves.

There are two kinds of softball. They are slow pitch or fast pitch. A slow-pitch team has ten players. A fast-pitch team has nine. In fast pitch, pitchers throw the ball fast. In fast pitch, players can bunt the ball and steal bases. Slow-pitch balls can be smaller than the fast-pitch balls.

Softball started in Chicago in 1887. It began as an indoor game. Later it was played outdoors.

Have you played softball? Give it a try!

Vocabulary

field: an area of open ground used to play a sport

inning: how baseball and softball games are divided; each team bats until getting three outs

Compare and Contrast

When reading "The Ball Game," compare and contrast baseball and softball and fast-pitch and slow-pitch softball. Complete the chart below.

Baseball	Softball
uses a smaller, harder ball	1.
2.	lasts seven innings
uses a bat, ball, and gloves	3.
throws the ball overhand	4.

Slow-pitch Softball	Fast-pitch Softball
ball thrown slowly	5.
6.	has nine players

Identify Main Idea and Supporting Details

Write the main idea of "The Ball Game" in the chart. Then, write small pieces of information that go along with the main idea, or the supporting details, in the chart.

Main Idea:

Supporting Detail 1:

Supporting Detail 2:

Supporting Detail 3:

Supporting Detail 4:

Comprehension Practice

Circle the letter of the best answer.

1. How is the ball thrown in softball?
   A. overhand
   B. underhand
   C. overhead
   D. sideways

2. How many innings does a softball game have?
   A. four
   B. five
   C. six
   D. seven

3. Where was softball started?
   A. New York City
   B. Philadelphia
   C. Chicago
   D. Los Angeles

4. In which year was softball started?
   A. 1832
   B. 1887
   C. 1920
   D. 1952

5. The main point of this article is to show what?
   A. that baseball is better than softball
   B. that baseball has nine innings
   C. that softball has slow pitch and fast pitch games
   D. that softball is different from baseball

6. In both baseball and softball, what is true about an **inning**?
   A. it lasts until there are three outs
   B. it is a type of bat
   C. it is the field where the game is played
   D. it lasts until someone scores a run

7. What is one difference between softball and baseball?
   A. Gloves are used only in baseball.
   B. There are a different number of bases.
   C. Softballs are bigger than baseballs.
   D. A softball game has more innings than baseball.

8. Which of these sentences is NOT true?
   A. There are two different kinds of softball.
   B. A softball field is smaller than a baseball field.
   C. Softball started as an indoor game.
   D. A baseball game has seven innings.

     © Teacher Created Materials

The Lady with the Lamp

Long ago, hospitals were different than they are today. Many were very dirty. They were full of diseases. Many patients died there. But Florence Nightingale wanted to change that.

Florence Nightingale was born in 1820. She liked books. She liked taking care of sick people. She decided to become a nurse. She went to nursing school. She was a good student.

Before Reading

- What is a hospital?
- What does a nurse do?

During Reading

- What were hospitals like long ago?
- Who was Florence Nightingale?

After Reading

- What important change did Florence Nightingale make?
- Would you like to be a nurse? Why or why not?

During a war, Florence ran a hospital for soldiers. At first, it was a huge, dirty barracks. Soldiers got very sick there. She worked hard to keep them from dying. She cleaned the place. At night, she carried a lamp to light her way as she worked. She became known as "the lady with the lamp." She saved thousands of lives. Then she became sick with a disease she got at a hospital.

Florence Nightingale became an expert in the care of the sick. People from all over the world came to her for advice. She is known as the founder of modern nursing.

Vocabulary

hospital: a place where sick people are cared for

barracks: a building in which soldiers live

founder: a person who starts or creates something

Identify Cause and Effect

As you read "The Lady with the Lamp," think about things that happen and why those things happen. Then complete the chart below.

What Happens (Effect)	Why It Happens (Cause)
1.	Long ago, hospitals were very dirty and full of diseases.
Florence Nightingale decided to become a nurse.	**2.**
Florence Nightingale became known as "the lady with the lamp."	**3.**
4.	Florence Nightingale became an expert in the field of nursing.

© *Teacher Created Materials*

Summarize and Paraphrase

When we read about something, we can summarize what we read by retelling it in our own words. After reading "The Lady with the Lamp," summarize what you read by retelling each paragraph in your own words.

Paragraph 1

Paragraph 2

Paragraph 3

Paragraph 4

Comprehension Practice

Circle the letter of the best answer.

1. When was Florence Nightingale born?
   A. 1820
   B. 1836
   C. 1920
   D. 1945

2. Florence Nightingale was a _____.
   A. doctor
   B. teacher
   C. soldier
   D. nurse

3. Who did Florence Nightingale run a hospital for?
   A. children
   B. animals
   C. soldiers
   D. teachers

4. Florence Nightingale is known as the founder of modern _____.
   A. medicine
   B. hospitals
   C. nursing
   D. schools

5. Why was Florence Nightingale called "The Lady with the Lamp"?
   A. She often worked at night and carried a lamp to see.
   B. She sold lamps to make extra money.
   C. She brought lamps to the soldiers so they could read.
   D. Her mother gave her a beautiful lamp.

6. What is the function of a **barracks**?
   A. it houses soldiers
   B. it gives free dental exams
   C. it is a place where soldiers eat
   D. it is a type of truck for carrying medical supplies

7. How did Florence Nightingale become a nurse?
   A. She went to work in a hospital.
   B. She nursed a sick family member.
   C. She went to nursing school.
   D. She took care of sick animals at home.

8. Why did people from all over the world come to Florence Nightingale?
   A. They wanted to see what she looked like.
   B. She was an expert on nursing.
   C. She was a good storyteller.
   D. They liked her personality.

Top of the World

Before Reading

- What is a mountain?
- Where is Hawaii?

During Reading

- Which mountain in the world is the highest above sea level?
- What is the tallest mountain in the world?

After Reading

- Who were the first people to climb Mount Everest?
- How do mountains grow?

Where is the top of the world?
The top of the world is Mount Everest. It is the highest mountain on Earth above sea level. It stands almost 30,000 feet (8,863 meters) high.

Has Mount Everest been climbed?
Yes. In 1953, two climbers made it to the top of Mount Everest. They were Edmund Hillary and Tenzing Norgay. Since then many climbers have reached the top.

What is the tallest mountain in the world?
The tallest mountain is Mauna Kea in Hawaii. It stands on the ocean floor. More than half of it is under water. It is 33,476 feet (10,203 meters) from the bottom to the top. Although it is technically taller than Mount Everest, it is not the highest because so little of it actually appears above sea level! That is why Mount Everest is technically the highest mountain in the world.

Do mountains grow?
Yes, some are growing. Rocks under the earth move. These rocks push up the mountains. Mount Everest grows every year. Some get smaller over time. Rain washes rocks off the top. This makes the mountains lower.

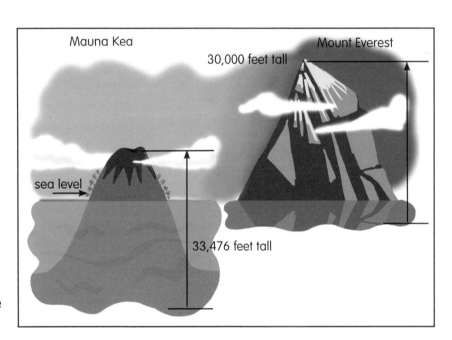

Mauna Kea

Mount Everest

30,000 feet tall

sea level

33,476 feet tall

Vocabulary

ocean floor: the bottom of the ocean

wash: to push downhill using flowing water

Identify Cause and Effect

As you read "Top of the World," think about what causes mountains to grow and what causes them to get smaller. Then complete the chart.

Cause	Effect
1.	Mountains grow and get higher.
2. Rain washes rocks off a mountain.	

 © Teacher Created Materials

Use Text Organizers

Headings can be helpful when you want to recall information that you have read. Read each section heading below from "Top of the World." Then tell what information you remember from that section.

1. "Where is the top of the world?"

_____

2. "Has Mount Everest been climbed?"

_____

3. "What is the tallest mountain in the world?"

_____

4. "Do mountains grow?"

_____

Use the text and pictures from "Top of the World" to answer the questions below.

5. Which is greater—the distance from the bottom of Mauna Kea to the top of Mauna Kea or the distance from the bottom of Mount Everest to the top of Mount Everest?

_____

_____

6. Which is higher above sea level—the top of Mount Everest or the top of Mauna Kea?

_____

_____

Comprehension Practice

Circle the letter of the best answer.

1. About how tall is Mount Everest?
   A. 10,000 feet (3,048 meters)
   B. 20,000 feet (6,096 meters)
   C. 30,000 feet (8,863 meters)
   D. 40,000 feet (12,192 meters)

2. Mount Everest was first climbed about how many years ago?
   A. 30
   B. 60
   C. 100
   D. 40

3. How far is it from the bottom of Mauna Kea to the top?
   A. 33,476 feet (10,203 meters)
   B. 63,476 feet (19,347 meters)
   C. 103,000 feet (31,394 meters)
   D. 40,004 feet (12,193 meters)

4. What happens to Mount Everest every year?
   A. It gets colder.
   B. It gets smaller.
   C. It gets higher.
   D. It gets wider.

5. Why is Mount Everest called "The Top of the World"?
   A. It is at the North Pole.
   B. It is covered with snow.
   C. It is taller than Mauna Kea.
   D. It is the highest mountain on Earth.

6. When rain **washes** rocks down a mountain, what happens to them?
   A. The mountains move.
   B. The mountains become smaller.
   C. The mountains grow on the ocean floor.
   D. They wear raincoats.

7. Where do we find information about which mountain is taller than Mount Everest?
   A. "What is the tallest mountain in the world?"
   B. "Where is the top of the world?"
   C. "Do mountains grow?"
   D. "Has Mount Everest been climbed?"

8. What causes some mountains to grow?
   A. Rain falling makes them grow.
   B. Rocks wash down and make them grow.
   C. Rocks move under the earth and push the mountains up.
   D. No one knows why mountains grow.

 © *Teacher Created Materials*

Martin Luther King, Jr.

Dr. Martin Luther King, Jr., was a great man. King led the fight for equal rights for African-Americans.

Dr. King was born on January 15, 1929, in Georgia. King's mother was a teacher. His father was a minister. Dr. King was smart. He started college when he was 15!

For a long time, African-Americans and white people were not treated the same. African-Americans were kept apart from white people. They could not go to the same schools. They could not eat at the same places.

Before Reading

- What are "rights"?
- Who is Martin Luther King, Jr.?

Dr. King worked for the rights of African-Americans. He wanted all people to be treated the same. He got many people to work together.

Dr. King wrote a great speech called "I Have a Dream." He told people how he felt. He wanted to make changes.

During Reading

- Were African-Americans treated the same as white people?
- What is the name of Dr. King's famous speech?

Many people did not want these changes. Not everyone was nice to Dr. King.

Dr. King was killed when he was just 39 years old. Each year, the United States remembers him on Martin Luther King, Jr. Day in January. Americans think about the great things he did!

After Reading

- What did Dr. King do to help African-Americans?
- Why should all people be treated fairly?

Vocabulary

minister: a person in charge of a church

rights: privileges given to people by the law

speech: a talk that is given to a group of people

Identify Author's Purpose and Viewpoint

Stories can be written for many different reasons. They can be written to inform, describe, entertain, or even teach a lesson to the reader. When you know why the story is written, it will help you understand and remember what you have read.

"Martin Luther King, Jr." was written for a reason. It was written to inform, or to give information, about something or someone. Read the story again. Decide what the author wanted you to learn about. Find three reasons to support your answer. Write your answers below.

This article gives information about: _____

Reason 1: _____

_____

_____

Reason 2: _____

_____

_____

Reason 3: _____

_____

_____

 #50089 Reading Comprehension—Level D © Teacher Created Materials

Identify Main Idea and Supporting Details

Read "Martin Luther King, Jr." again. Pick out the main idea and find three supporting details. Write your answers in the chart.

Main Idea:

Supporting Detail 1:

Supporting Detail 2:

Supporting Detail 3:

Comprehension Practice

Circle the letter of the best answer.

1. Where was Martin Luther King, Jr., born?
   A. Illinois
   B. Florida
   C. Georgia
   D. Washington

2. What did Martin Luther King, Jr., fight for?
   A. equal rights for African-Americans
   B. lower gas prices
   C. African-Americans to remain separate
   D. longer school days

3. What is the name of Dr. King's famous speech?
   A. "I Have Something to Say"
   B. "Listen to Me"
   C. "You Want to Hear This"
   D. "I Have a Dream"

4. What was Dr. King's dream?
   A. All people would be treated equally.
   B. People would stay separate.
   C. African-Americans would be treated better than others.
   D. African-Americans would have fewer rights.

5. What is the purpose of Martin Luther King, Jr. Day?
   A. to go to sales in shopping malls
   B. to learn the art of making speeches like Dr. King
   C. to have a day off from school
   D. to celebrate the great things Dr. King did

6. What is an example of a **right** that African-Americans were not allowed in Dr. King's time?
   A. They could not go to the same schools as white people.
   B. They could not eat at the same places as white people.
   C. They were not treated equally with white people.
   D. All of the above

7. Which statement best describes why the author wrote this story?
   A. Everyone agreed with everything that Dr. King said.
   B. Dr. King lived to be 80 and accomplished so much.
   C. Dr. King was an important man who changed the world.
   D. African-Americans fought against Dr. King.

8. How old was Dr. King when he died?
   A. 39   C. 15
   B. 50   D. He is still alive.

George Washington

George Washington was America's first president. He was important. Washington was born on February 22, 1732. He lived in Virginia. He had five brothers and sisters.

In school, math was George's best subject. He stopped going to school at age 15. This was not unusual at the time.

George had many jobs when he was young. He was a soldier. He worked as a farmer. He had other jobs too.

In 1759, he married his wife Martha. She had been married before. She had two children. George and Martha did not have children of their own.

George took a new job in 1775. He led Americans in the Revolutionary War. They won the war. America became its own country.

In 1789, George was elected president of the United States. He was 57 years old. George was president for eight years.

When George died, the capital of the United States was moved near his home. It is called Washington, D.C., and is named after George!

Have you seen his face on a U.S. dollar bill?

Before Reading

- What is a president?
- What does a president do?

During Reading

- How long was Washington president?
- What is named after Washington?

After Reading

- Why was Washington important?
- Would you want to be a president? Why or why not?

Vocabulary

president: person elected to be in charge of a country

capital: a city that holds the government of a country or state

country: a nation that is independent

Ask Questions

As you read, you may discover that you have questions about what you are reading. In this selection, you learned about George Washington. Do you have questions about what you read? Below are three different topics about George Washington. The topics come from the story. Write a question you might have for each of the topics.

Topic 1: George Washington's Childhood

Question:

_____

_____

_____

Topic 2: The Revolutionary War

Question:

_____

_____

_____

Topic 3: Washington as President

Question:

_____

_____

_____

Summarize and Paraphrase

When you write a summary, you understand and remember what you read because you have to think about important information in the story. Reread the selection on George Washington. Then write a summary on what you have learned about George Washington.

George Washington

_____

_____

_____

_____

_____

_____

_____

_____

_____

_____

_____

_____

_____

_____

_____

Comprehension Practice

Circle the letter of the best answer.

1. How long was George Washington president?
   A. two years
   B. four years
   C. six years
   D. eight years

2. What was one of the important things Washington did?
   A. helped win the Revolutionary War
   B. built his own house
   C. invented the first car
   D. bought the country of England

3. What important place was named after George Washington?
   A. New York
   B. Washington, D.C.
   C. Georgia
   D. Virginia

4. Where can we see George Washington's picture every day?
   A. in the photo album at your house
   B. in his high school yearbook
   C. on the U.S. dollar bill
   D. on the cover of a cereal box

5. What is the main reason we remember George Washington?
   A. He is named after the capital of our country.
   B. He was the first president of the United States.
   C. He was very good at math.
   D. He lived a long time ago.

6. Washington D.C. is the **capital** of our country. What does that mean?
   A. It is the center of our government.
   B. Everything there begins with a capital letter.
   C. The people live there.
   D. All of the above

7. George Washington led the Revolutionary War so that _____.
   A. his city could become the capital
   B. his face could be on the dollar bill
   C. the United States could be its own country
   D. he could be president

8. Which question could be asked about George Washington's personal life?
   A. How does someone become president?
   B. What did he do to help win the war?
   C. When was Washington, D.C., named?
   D. How many children did he have?

 © *Teacher Created Materials*

Comprehension Review:
Vocabulary—Word Meaning

Read each sentence. Use the information in the sentence to choose the meaning for the underlined word. Mark the answer.

1. Look both ways before you cross the <u>street</u>.
   A. crosswalk
   B. park
   C. road
   D. letter

2. The <u>vertical</u> line runs from top to bottom.
   A. colored
   B. slanted
   C. straight across
   D. straight up and down

3. The <u>gem</u> in the ring was a small diamond.
   A. metal
   B. jewel
   C. shell
   D. rock

4. The <u>journey</u> across the country took a long time.
   A. location
   B. transportation
   C. long trip
   D. road

5. The Earth <u>revolves</u> around the sun once a year.
   A. circles
   B. completes
   C. reaches
   D. faces

Comprehension Review:
Vocabulary—Opposites

Read each sentence. Choose the word that means the opposite of the underlined word. Mark the answer.

1. The trail was <u>rough</u> and bumpy.
   - **A.** rocky
   - **B.** smooth
   - **C.** hard
   - **D.** uneven

2. Lemons taste <u>sour</u> to most people.
   - **A.** bitter
   - **B.** salty
   - **C.** tart
   - **D.** sweet

3. The <u>ugly</u> caterpillar would one day be a butterfly.
   - **A.** beautiful
   - **B.** good
   - **C.** sad
   - **D.** bad

4. Alligators have short, <u>strong</u> legs.
   - **A.** long
   - **B.** weak
   - **C.** evil
   - **D.** powerful

5. An insect's abdomen is the <u>hind</u> part of its body.
   - **A.** top
   - **B.** back
   - **C.** front
   - **D.** short

  © *Teacher Created Materials*

Comprehension Review:
Vocabulary—Content Clues

Read each sentence. Use the information in the sentence to choose the best word to complete the sentence. Mark the answer.

1. We found it difficult to climb up the very ____ hill.
   A. low
   B. dry
   C. steep
   D. flat

2. The ____ included goods being shipped from China.
   A. travelers
   B. freight
   C. airplane
   D. note

3. A ____ is a reptile without legs.
   A. snake
   B. lizard
   C. turtle
   D. crocodile

4. Oysters ____ pearls by covering sand with nacre.
   A. hide
   B. create
   C. eat
   D. plant

5. The Pacific is the world's largest ____.
   A. lake
   B. continent
   C. piece of land
   D. ocean

Comprehension Review:
Sentence Completion

One word does not fit in the sentence. Use the sentence clues to choose that word. Mark the word that does NOT fit.

1. James _____ a bird flying to a nest in a pine tree.
   - **A.** saw
   - **B.** noticed
   - **C.** observed
   - **D.** told

2. Mac did not want people throwing _____ on the beach.
   - **A.** litter
   - **B.** trash
   - **C.** garbage
   - **D.** balls

3. You must _____ the toenails so that they are shorter.
   - **A.** polish
   - **B.** cut
   - **C.** clip
   - **D.** trim

4. The Earth and other planets _____ around the sun.
   - **A.** circle
   - **B.** orbit
   - **C.** center
   - **D.** revolve

5. To prepare for the spelling test, I _____ the spelling words.
   - **A.** studied
   - **B.** ignored
   - **C.** reviewed
   - **D.** learned

Comprehension Review:
Main Idea

Read each story. Mark the sentence that tells the main idea.

1. Australia has some unusual mammals. Platypuses live in Australia. They are one of only two kinds of mammals that lay eggs. Kangaroos are from Australia. They are one of a few kinds of mammals that carry their young in pouches.

   A. Platypuses live in Australia.

   B. They are one of only two kinds of mammals that lay eggs.

   C. Australia has some unusual mammals.

   D. Kangaroos are from Australia.

2. Many people think of mice when they hear the word <u>rodent</u>. However, mice are not the only rodents. Squirrels are rodents. Beavers are rodents, and so are porcupines. Many different kinds of gnawing animals are rodents.

   A. Many people think of mice when they hear the word <u>rodent</u>.

   B. Many different kinds of gnawing animals are rodents.

   C. Squirrels are rodents.

   D. Beavers are rodents, and so are porcupines.

3. Adult rabbits and hares look a lot alike, but newborns are very different. Newborn hares have hair. Rabbits are born without hair. Rabbits are born blind, but hares have their eyes open at birth.

   A. Rabbits are born blind, but hares have their eyes open at birth.

   B. Rabbits are born without hair.

   C. Adult rabbits and hares look a lot alike, but newborns are very different.

   D. Newborn hares have hair.

Comprehension Review:
Stated Details

Read the paragraph. Use the information in the paragraph to complete the sentences. Mark the answer.

Sir Walter Raleigh was an English explorer, soldier, and writer in the late 1500s and early 1600s. He was also a good friend of Queen Elizabeth I of England. According to one story, Raleigh was once visiting the queen at her court. They were out walking. When they reached a large puddle, the queen stopped. Ever the gentleman, Raleigh took off his coat. He spread it on the ground, so the queen could walk on it. He didn't want the queen to get her feet or clothes wet. No one knows if this story is true. We do know that Raleigh and the queen were friends. She made him a knight in 1585. She gave him a large piece of land in Ireland. He, in turn, helped the English defeat the Spanish at sea in 1588. He also sent colonists to North America in the 1580s. The two colonies set up on Roanoke Island did not succeed.

1. Sir Walter Raleigh was a friend of Queen _____.

   A. Mary   **B.** Elizabeth I   **C.** Anne   **D.** Elaine

2. In _____, the queen made Raleigh a knight.

   A. 1580   **B.** 1585   **C.** 1588   **D.** 1590

3. According to one story, Raleigh took off his coat so that _____.

   A. the queen could walk on it   **C.** he wouldn't be hot

   B. he could use it as a pillow   **D.** the queen could wear it

4. Raleigh did not succeed in setting up colonies in _____.

   A. England   **B.** Spain   **C.** North America   **D.** Ireland

5. The queen gave Raleigh a large piece of land in _____.

   A. England   **B.** Spain   **C.** North America   **D.** Ireland

Comprehension Review: Classify/Categorize

Read each group of words. Mark the word that does not fit in the same category as the other words.

1. A. colored pencils
    B. markers
    C. paper clips
    D. crayons

2. A. mitten
    B. sock
    C. shoe
    D. boot

3. A. chicken
    B. duck
    C. goose
    D. horse

4. A. Asia
    B. Europe
    C. North America
    D. Bolivia

5. A. violet
    B. pine
    C. daffodil
    D. tulip

6. A. moose
    B. elk
    C. dolphin
    D. deer

7. A. chair
    B. desk
    C. bench
    D. stool

8. A. knees
    B. nose
    C. eyes
    D. mouth

9. A. lunch
    B. dinner
    C. milk
    D. breakfast

10. A. atlas
    B. globe
    C. almanac
    D. dictionary

Comprehension Review: Sequence

Read the paragraph. Then answer the questions that ask about sequence.

How do grapes become raisins in a box on the grocery shelf? First, seedless grapes are allowed to ripen on the vine. Then they are picked. Workers lay the bunches of grapes on thick paper between the rows of grape plants. The grapes are allowed to dry in the sun for about two weeks. Then the dried grapes are kept in large bins for a while before they are sent to a packing house. At the packing house, the raisins are removed from the stems. They are separated by size. Then they are cleaned. Finally, they are packaged.

1. What happens to the grapes right before they are allowed to dry in the sun?
   A. Workers lay the grapes on rows of paper between the plants.
   B. The grapes are kept in bins.
   C. The grapes are separated by size.
   D. The grapes are packaged.

2. What is the first step in preparing raisins?
   A. removing grapes from the stem
   B. washing the grapes
   C. allowing grapes to ripen on the vine
   D. packaging the grapes

3. What happens to the grapes right after they are dried for about two weeks?
   A. They are placed between rows of grapevines.
   B. They are placed in large bins for a while.
   C. They are immediately cleaned.
   D. They ripen.

4. What is the last step in preparing the raisins for the market?
   A. The dried grapes are sized.
   B. The raisins are packaged.
   C. The grapes are removed from their stems.
   D. The grapes are picked.

    © Teacher Created Materials

Comprehension Review: Plot, Setting, Characters

Read the selection. Use the information to answer the questions. Mark the answer.

Chase is his baseball team's best pitcher. He can throw the ball really fast. However, Chase is the worst hitter. Everyone hits better than he does. Mike is the team's best hitter. Today, Chase's team needs just one run to win the game. It's Mike's turn to bat. Everyone thinks he will get a home run and win the game. Mike walks up to home plate and does a practice swing. He is sure he can hit the ball out of the park to win. A pitch is thrown, and Mike swings and misses. "Strike one!" the umpire calls. A second pitch is thrown, and Mike misses. No one can believe it when Mike swings at the last pitch and misses. Mike strikes out! Chase groans. He is next at bat. It is up to him. If he doesn't get a hit, the game will be over, and his team will lose. Chase drags his bat as he slowly walks to home plate. He doesn't even swing at the first pitch. He swings at the second pitch and misses. Chase looks at his teammates. He hates to disappoint them. He will try his best to hit the ball and get to first base. Then maybe the next batter can get a hit. The pitch is thrown. Chase swings and hears a crack. He begins to run to first base as he watches the ball. It flies over the fence. Chase can't believe it. He hit a home run. The crowd cheers, and his team waits for him at home plate. He is the hero of today's game.

1. Where and when does the story take place?
   A. backyard today
   B. ballpark on Saturday
   C. backyard on Saturday
   D. ballpark today

2. Who is the main character?
   A. the umpire
   B. Mike
   C. Chase
   D. the team

3. Who does everyone think will win the game for the team?
   A. the umpire
   B. Mike
   C. Chase
   D. Anthony

4. How many runs does the team need to win the game?
   A. one
   B. two
   C. three
   D. four

Comprehension Review:
Predict

Read each paragraph. Use the information to predict what will happen. Mark the answer.

1. On Saturday, Sean does his errands in the morning after he runs. He usually goes to the bank, the cleaners, and the grocery store. He has already been to the bank and the grocery store. Where will he go next?
   - **A.** bank
   - **B.** running
   - **C.** cleaners
   - **D.** department store

2. Jackie is cleaning her goldfish bowl. She took the fish out and put it in a cup of water. Then she poured out the water. She filled the sink with soapy water. What will she do next?
   - **A.** put the fish back in the bowl
   - **B.** put the bowl in the soapy water
   - **C.** add fresh water to the fishbowl
   - **D.** dry the fishbowl

3. David enjoys reading the newspaper in the morning. Every day, the paper is delivered to his house. He goes outside and picks the paper up. He opens the paper and sits down at the table. What will David do next?
   - **A.** David reads the paper.
   - **B.** David leaves for work.
   - **C.** David puts the paper in the recycling bin.
   - **D.** David watches television.

4. Barbara bought a ticket. She went into the theater and found a seat. She watched commercials for movies coming to the theater in a few weeks. What did Barbara do next?
   - **A.** She left the theater.
   - **B.** She watched the movie.
   - **C.** She sat down.
   - **D.** She made a phone call.

© Teacher Created Materials

Comprehension Review: Make Inferences

Read the sentences. Use the information to make inferences. Mark your answer.

1. Anton chose some sweet oranges. Then he took a box of cereal and a loaf of bread. He also put some cheese in his basket. He paid for the food and then carried it home in a bag. Where did Anton shop?
   A. clothing store
   B. bookstore
   C. grocery store
   D. a restaurant

2. Kate was reading a story and came to a word that she did not know. She asked her mom what the word meant. Mom told Kate to look the word up. That's exactly what she did. Now Kate knows the meaning of the word. Where did Kate look to find the meaning of the word?
   A. on a menu
   B. in a dictionary
   C. in the telephone book
   D. in a magazine

3. Emily saw a small animal. It had more than four legs. Insects and spiders have more than four legs. It had three body parts. Insects have three body parts. It had wings. Insects and birds have wings. It had antennae. Insects and lobsters have antennae. What kind of animal did Emily see?
   A. spider
   B. bird
   C. lobster
   D. insect

4. Juan had studied very hard. He had wanted to get an "Excellent" on the test. The test was handed back to him today. Juan smiled. What grade did Juan get on the test?
   A. Excellent
   B. Very Good
   C. Good
   D. Not Good

Comprehension Review: Cause and Effect

Read each sentence. Mark the cause or effect for the sentence.

1. Mia dropped the glass vase. What is the effect?
   A. The vase was filled with flowers.
   B. The vase broke into pieces.
   C. The vase bounced up and down.
   D. Mia put the vase on the table.

2. All the streets, sidewalks, and lawns are wet. What is the cause?
   A. It has rained.
   B. The temperature is low.
   C. The town has been cleaned.
   D. It is icy outside.

3. Josh forgot to turn on the oven. What is the effect?
   A. The oven was hot.
   B. The muffins did not bake.
   C. The muffins burned.
   D. The kitchen got very warm.

4. Elena got a ribbon for coming in first in the race. What was the cause?
   A. Elena did not run in the race.
   B. One runner finished the race before Elena.
   C. Elena won the race.
   D. Elena lost the race.

5. The soup was too hot to eat. What was the effect?
   A. Raul heated the soup some more.
   B. Raul threw the soup away.
   C. Raul put the soup bowl in the sink.
   D. Raul let the soup get cooler.

© Teacher Created Materials